ANXIETY GONE:

THE THREE C's OF ANXIETY RECOVERY

STANLEY HIBBS, PH.D.

Anxiety Gone: The Three C's of Anxiety Recovery

Published by Dare2Dream Books, Mustang, Oklahoma
405-642-8257

Printed in the United States of America by
Dare2Dream Books

Library of Congress Cataloging-in-Publication Data
A catalog record for this book is
Available from the Library of Congress

ISBN: 978-0-9779689-3-0

Acknowledgements

This is my second book. As recently as six years ago, I would have never thought it possible that I would ever write even one book. What would I write about? How would I ever find the time? But I prayed to be able to write a book, and somehow God made it happen, not once but twice. I will be eternally grateful for this.

On a more earthly level, I am grateful to my editor at Dare2Dream Books, Dr. Jim Morris. He and I have never met face to face, but I feel that I have gotten to know him well. His careful editing, encouraging feedback, and gentle prodding have played a big part in the completion of this book.

I am grateful to Jeff Galloway for his speedy and yet very creative cover design. I also appreciate the advice and feedback from my friend and marketing guru, Jay Rowland.

I also want to thank my wife, Suzanne, for her invaluable assistance. She has always been in my corner and has managed the details of our family life, while I slogged my way through the writing process. In addition, she is the best proofreader I have ever seen! I will carefully craft a page of text and believe it to be "perfect," only to be humbled when she finds a host of typos.

Finally, I want to thank the many clients who have trusted me with their care. It takes courage to open your heart to a complete stranger, but so many wonderful people have been willing to do just that. It has been a privilege to accompany you on the road to more abundant living.

TABLE OF CONTENTS

Chapter One

YOU DON'T HAVE TO SUFFER

Although you and I may never meet, there are a few things that I already know about you. You want to live life to the fullest. You want to succeed. You want to enjoy the companionship of family and friends. You want to be free to make rational and thoughtful decisions about what really matters to you. You want to feel relaxed and confident as you go about your daily activities.

Sadly, if you are like millions of people today, you may have an enemy that is keeping you from being all that you could be. That enemy is anxiety—unreasonable, irrational and unnecessary anxiety. Anxiety has different names such as fear, worry, and panic; but they're all basically the same thing. In over 25 years of practice as a psychologist, I have seen fear in many forms: worry, panic attacks, phobia, social anxiety, and obsessive-compulsive disorder. Here are a few real-life examples of anxiety. All of these clients had little faith that their problems could be helped, but all experienced significant recovery from their anxiety problems. Of course, I have changed their names and the details of their situations in order to protect their confidentiality.

Allow me to introduce Elizabeth. She was in her early 50's but acted like she was well over 70. She was convinced that she was "falling apart" physically and mentally. Although her physician had ruled out any medical conditions, she felt sure that something was wrong with her heart, and even the slightest physical exertion might kill her. Because of her fear, she spent much of her day in bed.

Elizabeth also avoided stairs because climbing caused her heart rate to increase. If she had to climb stairs, she would go up a few steps but then would feel anxious. She might then sit down and catch her breath before going up a couple more steps. At this extremely slow pace, it might take her several hours to climb one flight of stairs. Elizabeth suffered from Panic Disorder with Agoraphobia.

Paul was afraid of people. Although a very bright and articulate man, he always feared that people were judging him. He avoided working outside because he feared that his neighbors disapproved of how he kept up his yard. He didn't go to church because he only owned two suits, and he feared that people would judge him because of his clothes. Paul's difficulties were consistent with what is called Social Anxiety Disorder.

Susan also suffered from Social Anxiety Disorder, but her symptoms were different. Susan dreaded business meetings or calling on clients. She also tried to avoid any situation in which she had to report to her colleagues.

Carl was 19 years old. Except for school, Carl had not been physically separated from his parents for four years. Previous therapists had reasonably assumed Carl's problems were symptom of some deeper family problem. However, these possible issues were explored in depth, but Carl still couldn't stand to be away from his parents. After meeting with him a few times, his problem became clear to me. Carl was suffering from Panic Disorder with Agoraphobia. It wasn't that he was too attached to his parents. It was just that when he was away from his parents, he tended to have panic attacks.

Mary worked for a nonprofit agency. Although she always received good performance reviews, she was constantly worrying about losing her job. And, if she lost her job, she worried that she wouldn't find another one and would end up on the street. Although her health was good, she constantly worried that she would become seriously ill. Even her religious faith, which should have been a source of comfort and reassurance, caused her to worry that she wasn't living the right kind of life. Mary suffered from Generalized Anxiety Disorder.

Barbara is in her early 70's. She has been happily married for 50 years and raised three children who are all doing well. Barbara has a charmed life. Her husband is retired from a very successful career. They play golf, play bridge, and regularly visit their beach house. Barbara is a bright, energetic woman who is dearly loved by her family and friends. But, Barbara has suffered from Obsessive-Compulsive Disorder (OCD) since she was eight years old. For most of her life, Barbara has been burdened by frightening thoughts about harm coming to her or to her family. For example, Barbara would not prepare food if there were any cleaning products in the vicinity. Even walking past a closed box of laundry detergent would cause her to throw out food that she had taken hours to prepare.

All of these individuals experienced significant recovery from their anxieties. The main component of their treatment was Cognitive-Behavioral Therapy (CBT). They didn't get better because I'm such a good therapist. They got better because the principles of CBT work.

Maybe you don't have much faith in "therapy." Maybe your vision of psychological treatment is spending years on the couch, reciting all of the woes of your childhood. CBT is not like that at all. It's more like a coaching or mentoring relationship in which the therapist teaches you easy-to-understand skills, which you practice between sessions. It's hard work for both therapist and client, but CBT is changing people's lives for the better.

In this book, I distill the essential features of CBT and present them in a systematic manner, which you can use to attack your own anxiety problems. Many of these concepts can be used without the need for professional therapy. However, if you are currently seeing a therapist who uses CBT, this book can be a helpful companion to your treatment.

As you will see, all anxiety recovery involves three basic activities. I call these the "Three C's of Anxiety Recovery." They are (1) Calm your body, (2) Correct your thinking, (3) Confront your fears. If you can apply these basic skills, you will be well on your way to overcoming your anxiety problems.

There are a number of excellent books on anxiety. However, many of them are quite lengthy, complicated, and filled with technical jargon. There is a need for a simple, easy-to-read handbook that clearly explains what anxiety is and how we can overcome it. This book is intended to fill that need.

Chapter Two

MOTIVATION FOR CHANGE

If you are prone to excessive anxiety and worry, it's probably difficult to imagine that you could get better. By this time, you may have resigned yourself to the limitations that your anxiety places on you.

Maybe you suffer from social anxiety. If so, what social situations do you avoid? Maybe you rationalize your isolation with comments like, "I really don't like parties anyway."

Did you used to dream of traveling, but your fear of flying has kept you from going anywhere? Maybe you justify missing out on travel with statements like, "I have everything I need close to home. Who needs to travel?"

Would you love to apply for a promotion at work, but the new position would require that you lead meetings and speak in front of groups? Maybe you gave up that idea a long time ago with thoughts like, "I couldn't possibly do that."

Have you long ago resigned yourself to the fact that, "I'm just a worrier," and there's nothing you can do about it?

I suggest that you take a chance and start to think differently. Try to imagine what your life would be like if you could master your anxiety. What would you do that you don't do now? What could you accomplish if you were not weighted down by your fears?

With all my clients, I ask them to write down a "payoff list." That is, I want them to write down ways in which their lives will be better when they conquer their anxiety. I ask them to make their payoffs as specific, detailed, and emotionally charged as possible. For example, "I have a better social life," is nice, but it might be too vague to motivate you to action. But something like, "I have the courage to ask that girl out that I have been admiring for months." Now, that's something that might get you going.

Throughout this book, I will describe specific **action steps** for you to take. Each step will be built on the previous one, so it's important to do them in order. Your success in overcoming your anxiety will depend on your willingness to take these action steps.

So, here's your first action step: Write down your own "payoff list." Write specific, detailed, and emotionally charged descriptions of how your life will be better when you have overcome your anxiety.

To help you out with this action step, here is a list of payoffs that my clients have used. Feel free to use any that fit for you. I include this list so you'll have a general idea what a "payoff" looks like. Notice that each "payoff" is written in the first person, present tense as if it were already true.

- I can go shopping at the mall whenever I want to, even by myself.

- I drive on the freeways as often as I want, so I can visit my friends all over the Southeast.

- I face new situations with courage and confidence and without a lot of worry. I make decisions based on logic and principle and not on fear.

- So I can take wonderful vacations and see places such as the Grand Canyon that I have always wanted to see, I am comfortable flying in airplanes.

- When I am out in public, I feel calm and confident. I go to any social event that I choose and don't miss out on things because I'm afraid.

- I can sit in business meetings and feel comfortable. I look forward to these meetings because I have something meaningful to contribute. I don't dread them or feel like I have to sit near the door, so I have a way to escape.

- I can do all the things that I used to avoid such as riding in elevators, taking public transportation, and going to crowded places because I have learned how to manage my panic attacks.

- I have a fuller life and make good use of my time because I no longer waste time engaging in useless rituals such as excessive hand washing, checking, or ordering.

- I am a great role model for my children because I have shown them that their lives don't have to be controlled by anxiety.

Again, use any of these examples that you would like, but make them your own. Modify them to suit your own particular needs. You might be tempted to skip this action step, but let me encourage you to take it. It will give you the motivation you need to see this process through to the end.

Chapter Three

ANXIETY UNPACKED

THE THREE C'S OF ANXIETY RECOVERY

There is one thing that I notice about my anxious clients: they are afraid of their fears. The state of anxiety is so uncomfortable, so overwhelming, or so mystifying that they will do almost anything to avoid being afraid. As their lives become governed by their fears, they lose the freedom to choose their own actions. These clients are afraid to experience even mild or moderate levels of anxiety for fear that it will escalate into extreme terror or panic.

The source of much of this fear is lack of knowledge. We are often afraid of what we don't understand, and people often have terribly inaccurate beliefs about what happens when they're anxious. They have thoughts such as, "I'm cracking up. I'm losing control. There's something terribly wrong with me. I'm going crazy. I'm having a nervous breakdown. I can't handle this. This is too much for me. I'll have a heart attack." All of these thoughts are grossly inaccurate and only serve to add to the fear.

One of the best ways to overcome anxiety is to understand it. We are going to demystify anxiety by breaking it down into its three components: the physical, the mental, and the behavioral.

The *physical* refers to what goes on in the body when we're anxious. You will learn exactly why these physical sensations take place. Why does your heart pound? Why do you have trouble breathing? There are perfectly logical reasons why these things happen in your body. And, you will learn how to effectively calm your body when you're anxious. In Chapter Four, we will explore the First "C" of Anxiety Recovery: *Calm your body.*

The *mental* refers to all the negative thoughts we have when we're anxious. You will learn that your thoughts are a major part of the problem. You are predicting disasters that will not happen and dreading catastrophes that will not be as bad as you think. You will learn that by changing your thinking, you can obtain a level of control over your anxiety that you never thought possible. In Chapter Five, we will explore the Second "C": *Correct your thinking.*

The *behavioral* refers to how anxiety impacts our actions and how our actions in turn contribute to anxiety. Because anxiety feels uncomfortable, we tend to avoid those situations that trigger anxious feelings. You will learn that avoiding things that make you anxious only makes the anxiety worse. You will be given psychological tools that will help you stop avoiding anxiety. Instead, you will learn how to confront and even embrace those situations that make you anxious. This will give you a level of personal freedom that you might not have believed possible. In Chapter Six, we will explore how to actively attack anxiety with the Third "C": *Confront your fears.*

Chapter Four

THE FIRST C OF ANXIETY RECOVERY: CALM YOUR BODY

The underlying purpose for all fear is to protect us from real danger. It alerts us to dangerous situations and prepares us for action. Healthy fear leads us to take reasonable precautions. It's partly out of fear that I wear seatbelts, look both ways before I cross the street, and get my annual medical checkup.

Healthy fear has probably saved many lives and insured the survival of the human race. To understand how this is so, let's go back in time to those prehistoric days when our human ancestors lived in the wild. Life was more physically dangerous then. Vulnerable human beings were easy prey for lions and tigers and bears—Oh my!

In such a world, survival was often dependent on the ability to flee to safety. Fortunately, we have a built-in emergency response system that automatically kicks in when we need to escape. Here's how that system works. The act of running requires rapid movement of large muscle groups in the legs, hips, and arms. For muscles to move, they need fuel. To get the fuel to where it's needed, the heart must pump faster and harder. This explains one of the most common physical symptoms of fear: rapid heartbeat.

In order to work well, the large muscle groups not only need blood; they also need oxygen. So, to get the oxygen to where it's needed, we must breathe fast and hard. This explains another common symptom of fear: rapid breathing or the feeling that we're not getting enough air.

As fuel is used up in the muscles, heat will be created. In order to regulate the body's temperature, we may start to perspire. Also, sweat on the skin makes us slippery and makes it harder for a predator to take hold. This explains another symptom: perspiration.

While we're running, the body is also preparing to defend itself. Thus, muscles tighten in preparation for battle. Thus, many anxious people experience muscle tension or tightness.

Since blood is needed in the deep muscle tissue, it tends to flow away from the skin. This may also help reduce bleeding if we are bitten. This flow of blood from the skin can create tingling or numbing sensations in the skin—another common physical symptom of fear.

During times of extreme danger, blood may actually flow away from the brain. There's no point in pondering the great truths of the universe, if we're running for our lives. This can create dizziness, light-headedness, and poor concentration that are often part of fear.

Finally, our digestion stops when we're in danger. After all, why digest our meat when any second we might *be* meat? This explains why we might experience nausea or a knot in our stomach when we're afraid.

Do you get the picture of what's happening? What goes on in your body would literally save your life if there were a tiger there. What's the obvious problem? There's no tiger.

In other words, your body has simply made a mistake. For reasons that we don't always understand, your emergency response system has been triggered. Your body is preparing for an emergency that isn't happening. To deal with the physical symptoms of anxiety, there are three facts that you must understand:

First, these physical symptoms are uncomfortable, but they are not harmful or dangerous in any way. You may **feel** like disaster has befallen you, but nothing bad is happening. You are not going crazy; you are not dying, and you're not losing control.

Of course, you would rather not have these physical sensations, but if you understand that they are harmless, perhaps that will make them endurable.

We often experience unpleasant physical sensations such as headaches, muscle soreness, and acid indigestion. We don't like these sensations, but because we label them as "normal," they don't bother us all that much.

I help my clients change their thinking about these physical sensations. Their old thoughts were something like, "Oh no, I'm getting anxious. I can't stand this. I have to make these sensations go away." Their new way of thinking is, "Here are those pesky sensations again. I can remind myself that there's nothing bad happening."

Second, these physical sensations are time-limited and will go away in due time. The emergency system cannot respond indefinitely. Once it's clear that there is no real danger, the body will return to its normal state.

In the throes of a panic attack, it's easy to believe that your fear will go on forever. It's not true. If you just ride it out, your discomfort will fade away.

Third, the physical sensations that accompany anxiety are similar to three other conditions: exercise, excitement and anger. When we engage in any strenuous physical exercise, our heartbeat increases, our breathing accelerates, and we perspire—just like a panic attack! The only difference is that we interpret the physical sensations differently. After jogging a mile, a rapidly beating heart doesn't bother us at all. In fact, it actually feels good. However, when we're not exercising, the same physical sensation triggers the inaccurate belief that something must be wrong with us.

Likewise, when we are excited, our body does many of the same things. Think about times when you've been excited. You're waiting for a loved one who's arriving on a plane. You're at a sporting event, and you're cheering on your favorite team. You are sexually attracted to someone. In each of these situations, you may notice your heart beating faster and your breathing rate increased. Again, these physical reactions are very similar to what happens during anxiety. But since the situation is positive, they don't trigger anxiety.

In a similar manner, anger triggers many of the same physical symptoms. You have probably heard of the "fight or flight" response. While fear represents the "flight," anger is the "fight," but physically they are quite similar.

Some of my clients experience enormous relief just from knowing these facts about anxiety. Many clients write out a brief summary of these ideas and regularly review them.

Here's an example: "There's no tiger. Nothing bad is happening. I am safe. These sensations are uncomfortable but they aren't dangerous, and they will pass in time."

Even though the physical sensations of anxiety are not dangerous, they are unpleasant, so it's helpful to have some techniques to control or eliminate them. This leads us to the First C of Anxiety Recovery: Calm your body. There are four activities that can be very helpful with this:

1. Deep abdominal breathing

2. Relaxation techniques

3. Visualization

4. Physical exercise

Deep Abdominal Breathing

Most people don't know this, but we have a natural tranquilizer that we can use any time. It is perfectly safe and has no side effects. It's called deep abdominal breathing. You may think you know how to breathe, but in reality most of us have "forgotten" how.

Watch a newborn baby breathe. Every time the baby inhales, its stomach will rise and then fall each time he exhales. Take that same child six years later, ask him to "take a deep breath," and you'll see something quite different. As the child inhales, his shoulders and chest will rise, but he will actually pull his stomach in—just the opposite of the newborn baby!

Millions of people have learned how relaxing and soothing it can be to return to the type of breathing we did as babies. It has been taught by everyone from yoga and meditation masters to behavioral psychologists. Take the time to master this technique, and you can instantly calm yourself no matter how stressful the situation.

Here's how to do it. Lie flat on your back. Place your right hand on your stomach, and your left hand on your chest. As you slowly breathe in, your right hand should rise while your left hand remains stationary. Breathe in to a slow count of three and then breathe out to a slow count of three. As you exhale, your right hand should slowly descend. Repeat this process for three to five minutes. You may get a little dizzy. If you do, don't worry; just slow down the process for a few minutes.

This may be harder than it sounds, but keep practicing and eventually you'll get it. Of course, consult your physician if you have any condition that might make it difficult to apply this skill. Once you have mastered the technique when you're lying on your back, you can start breathing this way while you're sitting up or standing.

Here's your next action step: Practice this simple breathing technique for 3-5 minutes twice a day. Practice it if you're anxious or if you're already perfectly calm. Learn how it feels. Don't wait until you're anxious to practice. Once you have developed your skill to calm your body, you can use this technique anytime you anticipate a stressful situation.

I use this technique all the time—in a room full of strangers, preparing to speak to a professional organization, or dealing with a conflict with someone I care about. I can instantly reduce my anxiety and create a greater sense of calm by taking just a few deep abdominal breaths. You can too!

Progressive Muscle Relaxation

There are a number of techniques that help calm and relax the body. Perhaps the best is progressive muscle relaxation. You can purchase professionally produced CD's that contain guided instruction on this technique. Or, you can create your own relaxation recording by reciting and recording the following instructions. If you would rather not have a recording of your own voice, you could ask a family member or friend to record it for you. The whole exercise takes about 10-15 minutes at most. Here are the instructions:

> "Make sure you are wearing loose comfortable clothing. Find a comfortable position. You can do this exercise either sitting up or stretched out on your back—whichever is more comfortable. In order to

eliminate visual distractions, close your eyes. Take a few deep abdominal breaths." (Pause a few seconds)

"During this exercise, try not to judge or evaluate your experience. Don't trouble yourself with thoughts such as, 'I wonder if I'm doing this right,' or 'I'm not getting relaxed enough.' Relaxation is a skill, and the more you practice the better you will become."

"With your right hand, make a fist and flex your bicep muscle. Hold that tension. (Wait about 8-10 seconds.) When those muscles are ready to relax, let them relax. Let your hand and arm return to a comfortable position. Notice the contrast between the tension and the relaxation. Be aware of something very important. You created the tension, and you created the relaxation. Continue to take deep abdominal breaths, and let yourself relax." (Wait about 15 seconds.)

"Now do the same thing with your left hand and arm. Make a fist and flex your bicep muscle. Hold that tension. (Wait about 8-10 seconds.) When the muscle is ready to relax, let it relax. Let your hand and arm return to a comfortable position. Again, notice the contrast between the tension and the relaxation. Continue to take deep, slow abdominal breaths, and just let yourself relax." (Wait about 15 seconds.)

"Now tighten up all the muscles of your face. Hold that tension. (Wait 8-10 seconds.) When those muscles are ready to relax, let them relax. Again, notice the contrast between the tension and the relaxation. Continue to take deep, slow abdominal breaths and just relax." (Wait about 15 seconds.)

"Now work on the tension in your neck, chest, and upper back by shrugging your shoulders up. Hold that tension. (Wait 8-10 seconds.) When those muscles are ready to relax, let them relax. Return to a relaxed, comfortable position. Again, notice the contrast between the tension and the relaxation. Continue to take deep, slow abdominal breaths, and just let yourself relax." (Wait about 15 seconds.)

"Now work to relax your stomach and lower back by arching your back up off of the chair—bed, sofa, floor, etc. Hold that tension. (Wait 8-10 seconds.) When those muscles are ready to relax, let them relax. Return to a relaxed, comfortable position. Again, notice the contrast between the tension and the relaxation. Continue to take slow, deep abdominal breaths, and just let yourself relax." (Wait about 15 seconds.)

"Now let's relax your right leg by stretching it out and pointing your toes away from your head. Hold that tension. (Wait 8-10 seconds.) When those muscles are ready to relax, let them relax. Stretch your right leg out again, but this time, stretch out your heel so that your toes point back toward your head. Hold that tension. (Wait 8-10 seconds.) When those muscles are ready to relax, let them relax. Notice the contrast between the tension and the relaxation. Continue to take slow, deep abdominal breaths, and just let yourself relax." (Wait about 15 seconds.)

"Now let's repeat this same procedure with the left leg. Stretch it out and point your toes away from your head. Hold that tension. (Wait 8-10 seconds.) When those muscles are ready to relax, let them relax. Now, stretch your left leg out but this time stretch out your heel so your toes point back toward your head. Hold that tension. (Wait 8-10 seconds.) When those muscles are ready to relax, let them relax. Again, notice the contrast between the tension and the relaxation."

"Continue to take deep slow breaths. If you notice any tension in your body, just take note of it and let it melt away."

Practice this exercise as often as you can—preferably once a day. Some people like to start their day with this exercise because it helps them dissipate any morning anxiety and gets them ready for the day. Other people like to do this exercise at night. They find it helpful in getting to sleep.

You may want to combine this relaxation exercise with the visualization exercise described below. Both techniques work together beautifully.

Visualization

Human beings have a remarkable ability to visualize things that are not actually present at the time. If you're at home, can you see the front of your workplace or school? Can you see the high school or college you attended? Can you "see" your favorite TV show?

There is something remarkable about visual images. Our body reacts to them as if they were "real." Think of the last time you saw a scary movie. You "knew" that you were watching images on a screen. You "knew" that these were actors playing a part. And yet, your emergency response system was likely triggered as if you were in the dangerous situation yourself. Your heart might have pounded; you might have held your breath; your muscles tensed, and you felt a knot in your stomach.

So, if visual images can trigger fear responses, they can also be used to calm the body and overcome anxiety. Here are the visualization instructions that I usually include with my relaxation exercises. Feel free to include them in your relaxation exercises as well.

"Now that your body is relaxed, we are going to calm the mind. I invite you to go on an imaginary trip. I invite you to go someplace where you always feel relaxed and peaceful. This can be anyplace you choose. It can be someplace that you have actually visited. Or, it can be a place that you create in your mind. It can be a combination of places. It is completely your choice." (Pause a few seconds.)

"Go to that special place and enjoy it as thoroughly as you can. What do you see there? Are you there by yourself, or are there people you care about nearby. Either way is OK. What colors do you see? What objects to you see? Everything you see and everything you experience will simply serve to help you become more and more relaxed. Make use of all of your senses. Are there any sounds in this place? Do you have any tactile sensations? Are there even any pleasant aromas associated with this place? (Pause about 30 seconds.)

"Once you have thoroughly explored this special, relaxing place, you can prepare yourself to leave it to return to this time and place. You won't be too reluctant to leave it because you know that this wonderful, relaxing place is inside you and you can return to it anytime you want. Every time you return to this place, you will become even more relaxed, calm, and peaceful."

All three interventions—deep breathing, relaxation, visualization—work well in combination with each other. If you practice these skills regularly, you will experience a reduction in your overall anxiety and stress; you will sleep better, and you will have greater confidence in your ability to tackle more serious anxiety problems.

Physical Exercise

In addition to regular use of deep breathing, progressive relaxation, and visualization, I strongly encourage my clients to engage in regular, physical exercise. I find that this helps them reduce their overall stress level and helps them make better use of all the techniques of CBT.

I realize that you have a busy schedule, so don't feel like you have to follow a very stringent and elaborate exercise program. I would rather you walk for ten minutes a day than to spend hundreds of dollars to join a fitness center that you never visit. Make it as simple and easy as possible. Just add a little physical activity to your daily schedule, and you'll be well rewarded with lower stress and more control over your anxiety problems.

Trusting Your Body

Chronically anxious individuals have learned to fear and mistrust their bodies. They are certain that any level of physical arousal means that "something terrible is happening." They may be afraid to get excited because they are uncomfortable with the physical sensations that accompany that feeling. They may be afraid to exercise for the same reason. <u>One of the most important skills in anxiety recovery is truly believing that physiological arousal is not harmful or dangerous</u>. Once you are truly convinced of this fact, you will be well on your way to overcoming your anxiety.

One way to develop more trust in your body is to purposely create some of the sensations that you fear. For example, if you are troubled by rapid heartbeat, do some "jumping jacks" or do a little jogging. That will get your heart going quite nicely, but it won't bother you because you'll be expecting it. Of course, if you have any medical conditions that make exercise a problem, you need to consult with your physician before trying this.

Other physical symptoms can be purposely created. Dizziness can be created by spinning around. Light-headedness can be simulated by breathing through a straw. I once had a woman client who experienced a pressure on her chest. I suggested that she do some exercises then lie on her back and place a heavy book on her chest. It worked like a dream.

Let me add a word of caution. If you have any concerns that these procedures will backfire and create more anxiety, do not do them on your own. Work with a trained cognitive-behavioral therapist who can coach you through these techniques appropriately.

I describe these techniques in order to illustrate this one essential principle for reducing anxiety: learn to trust your body and recognize that physical arousal is a benign phenomenon.

Medications

Although CBT is a very effective treatment for most anxiety problems, appropriate medications can often play an important role. The decision whether or not to try medication is an individual one and must be made in consultation with a psychiatrist or other physician.

Since I am not a physician, I always require my clients to look to their physician for guidance on appropriate medical intervention. There are some patients who will almost certainly require medication. These include:

1. The patient whose anxiety is so severe and debilitating that they cannot participate in CBT without at least "taking the edge off."

2. The patient is also suffering from significant depression.

3. Patients with severe obsessive-compulsive disorder.

Many physicians are concerned about the widespread use of the class of medications known as benzodiazepines. Some brand name examples are Valium, Xanax, and Ativan. These medications are fast acting, short-term anxiety relievers, that can be helpful in a crisis situation but can pose problems when used for long-term anxiety treatment. Since the patient experiences such immediate relief, there is the possibility of developing a dependence upon them. In addition, as the medication wears off, many patients experience a rebound effect of increased anxiety, which just encourages them to take more medicine.

You should carefully discuss your medication options with your physicians. Many physicians favor the use of antidepressant medications for certain anxiety conditions. These slower-acting, longer-acting medications do not pose such a risk of dependence.

Summing Up

All anxiety recovery begins with the First C: Calm your body. As you develop confidence in your understanding and control over your physical symptoms, you will be ready to move on to the Second C: Correct your thinking.

Chapter Five

THE SECOND C OF ANXIETY RECOVERY: CORRECT YOUR THINKING

Having learned how to deal with the physical side of anxiety, let's now turn to the mental or "cognitive" side of anxiety. The word "cognition" essentially means, "thinking." Practitioners of Cognitive-Behavioral Therapy (CBT) have noted that upsetting emotions, including anxiety, are always triggered by thoughts. These thoughts are often called Automatic Thoughts (AT's) because they occur so immediately, naturally, and habitually that we often do not even recognize them. Nevertheless, it is the AT's that determine what we feel in any situation. It is not the situation itself.

Here's an example. Suppose that I'm having lunch with a friend. In the midst of the conversation, I notice him yawning and staring at his watch. How might I feel then? Well, it depends on how I think.

If my Automatic Thoughts are, "How rude; He shouldn't act that way around a friend," I'll feel annoyed or angry. If my AT's are, "I'm boring him. He must be tired of talking with me," I might have hurt feelings. On the other hand, if my AT's are, "I wonder if he's tired or if he has something on his mind," I might feel concern for him.

So, it's not my friend's behavior that makes me feel a certain way, it's my **thoughts** about his behavior. If I didn't take the time to notice my thoughts, then I would just assume that my feelings were the **only right** feelings to have.

If you suffer from anxiety, you have developed certain habits of thinking (AT's), which significantly contribute to your problem.

The human brain is far more complex than any computer, so thoughts flow through our minds quickly and are gone before we notice them. However with practice, we can learn to identify our thoughts, determine how they might be flawed, and replace them with more helpful thoughts. Anxiety recovery is accomplished by:

1. Identifying our fearful thoughts;
2. Identifying how our thoughts are inaccurate or unhelpful;
3. Replacing our negative thoughts with more productive ones.

Identifying Our Fearful Thoughts

Perhaps the most important and yet most challenging aspect of CBT is helping the client identify what **thoughts** are contributing to his/her anxiety. So often the initial response is "I'm not thinking anything; I'm just afraid."

Marilyn was a delightful woman in her late 60's who had been struggling with anxiety for most of her life. In fact, she began almost every day with intense feelings of anxiety. When asked, "What are you anxious about?" she would strongly protest, "I don't know. I just feel a tremendous sense of dread."

Like I do with many of my clients, I asked Marilyn to read *The Feeling Good Handbook* by Dr. David Burns. This book describes the principles of CBT, and many of my clients have found it very helpful. However, Marilyn didn't find it helpful at all. In fact it made her anxious to read it. She just didn't see the relevance of her **thoughts** to her anxiety. "I'm not thinking about anything in particular; I just **feel** anxious!"

Fortunately, Marilyn was patient and continued in therapy while I struggled to find a way to help her. Finally, I came across an idea that made a difference. It all had to do with the anatomy of the brain.

I explained to Marilyn that different parts of the brain handle different functions. If you touch the side of your head just above your right ear, you'll be pointing at the limbic system. This is your "emotional brain." During times of strong emotion, the limbic system works overtime. The "emotional brain" reacts quickly, which doesn't allow time for a realistic assessment of the situation. For that, you have to involve other parts of the brain.

Now, if you touch your forehead between your eyes, you will be close to the prefrontal cortex. This area is associated with our language skills. We must access this "language brain," in order to have the words necessary to describe our experiences. Once the "language brain" gets turned on, the "emotional brain" becomes less active. That is, when we put our experiences into words, we begin to get control over our emotions.

But, that doesn't complete the process; once we have words to describe our experience, we then need to access the "problem solving brain." To find this, move your finger up from between your eyes and slightly to your left. You'll be pointing toward the frontal lobe of the cerebral cortex, the site of many of our problem solving skills.

If Marilyn had been a neuropsychologist, I am sure that she could have quibbled with my somewhat oversimplified version of the differences between the "emotional brain," "language brain," and "problem-solving brain." Nevertheless, these are helpful distinctions that many of my clients have found helpful.

So, this is what Marilyn and I did. I had her imagine that it was morning, and she was feeling very anxious. I understood that no mere words could ever clearly express the extent of her anxiety, but I urged her to do her best to put words to her fears. Specifically, I asked her to think about what "bad event" might happen. Her first responses were vague statements such as, "It's going to be a bad day."

Sticking with her, I asked, "I know this might be just a guess, but what will happen to make it a bad day?"

Finally, she began to be more specific. "I'll be bored. I won't have anything worthwhile to do. I'll be lonely because there will be no one around."

Now, we were getting somewhere! Rather than a vague sense of dread, her anxiety was clearly connected to feared "bad events." Now, we could apply some simple problem solving to help her deal with these "bad events." This was a turning point for Marilyn. Over the next few weeks, she was transformed from an anxious CBT skeptic into a calmer and self-confident woman.

Negative Fortune Telling

Cognitive-behavioral therapists have discovered that anxiety is almost always associated with the unfortunate mental habit of "negative fortune telling." That is, we are predicting that some bad event is going to happen. Once we clearly identify what the "bad event" is, we have taken the first important step in dealing with it.

Here's your next action step: Whenever you are anxious, do your best to put <u>words</u> to your fears. What

specific "bad event" are you predicting? Be sure to write these down.

You might find that your initial "bad events" are somewhat vague and poorly defined. For example, your "bad events" might consist of just more emotional reactions (E.g., "I'll be miserable all day. I won't be able to stand it.") If you have thoughts such as these, keep looking for a more specific outcome ("OK, if I'm going to be miserable all day, what will specifically happen to me?"). Keep questioning yourself in this way until you identify clearly defined "bad events." (E.g., "I won't get my work done. My co-workers will notice that I'm anxious," etc.)

Again, it's important to use your "language brain" to put words to your fears and connect them to specific "bad events."

Here are some examples of common specific "bad events."

- Some "bad events" will deal with issues surrounding your competence or ability.

  "I'll lose the client."
  "I'll be fired."
  "My business will fail."
  "I'll flunk out of college."

- Some "bad events" will involve the potential for social disapproval.

  "I'll make a fool of myself."
  "They'll think that I'm a loser."
  "I'll let them down."
  "They won't like me."

- Some "bad events" will involve unfortunate, but not fatal, outcomes.

  "I'll be late."

"I'll miss the meeting."
"We'll lose the game."
"I won't get my raise."

Challenging and Correcting Our Fearful Thoughts

Once you have clearly identified your thoughts and used your "language brain," to identify specific "bad events," you are prepared to challenge your negative thoughts. This will require the use of your "problem-solving brain." You might be surprised to learn that your fearful thinking is often quite flawed. Specifically, when we are anxious, we are usually engaging in one or more of the following mental errors:

1. We may be overestimating the likelihood that the bad thing will happen.

2. If the bad thing does happen, we may be overestimating how bad the consequences will be.

3. If the bad thing does happen, we may be underestimating our ability to cope with it.

So, once the "bad events" are identified, I always coach my clients to ask themselves a number of key questions:

"What is the real likelihood that the bad thing will happen?"

Often, we will be anxious about things that are very unlikely, if not impossible, to happen. I once worked with a graduate student who was deathly afraid of meeting with her faculty advisor. Her "bad event" was, "He'll laugh at me and tell me that I'm a lousy graduate student." Her grades were good. And although the faculty advisor was a bit cold and formal, he had never insulted her ability as a student.

Therefore, she had to conclude that there was virtually no chance that her advisor would act that way.

"Is there anything that is more likely to happen than the thing I'm afraid of?"

Often we are so focused on the possible "bad events" that we fail to remember that there might be other outcomes that are quite positive or at least neutral. So, make a point of reminding yourself of all the good things that might happen. Whenever I fly on an airplane, I always consider that very minute possibility of an accident. However, I quickly remind myself of the much more likely result that I'll get to my destination safely and thoroughly enjoy myself when I get there.

If we focus on the potential for positive outcomes, we might actually increase the chances that they will happen. For example, I have been a guest on radio talk shows on several occasions. I'm usually somewhat anxious prior to the program. My "fortune telling" thoughts are "I'll have nothing to say. I'll open my mouth and nothing will come out. I'll make a fool of myself." However, I always remind myself that I have usually done quite well in these situations, and the "bad events" have never happened. So, I prepare thoroughly and visualize myself doing a good job, which increases my chances of success.

Catastrophic Thinking

Here's another question to ask yourself.

"If the "bad thing" should happen, what would be the real consequences? What would it really mean to me?"

Human beings are prone to "catastrophic thinking." That is, we often tell ourselves that a certain outcome would be "terrible, awful, or the end of the world." In reality, although the feared "bad thing" is unwanted and unfortunate, it's often not nearly as bad as you might imagine.

I remember when one of my sons attended a private school that was over 20 miles from our home. Every morning, my job was to drive him to the bus stop. Since the school was so far away, I was always concerned that we would miss the bus, and I would end up driving him all the way to school.

The problem was that I was too concerned. Every morning, I would make myself a nervous wreck and become irritable at my wife and kids because I was so worried about missing that bus. Finally, it dawned on me that missing the bus would not be the end of the world. Yes, it would be inconvenient and pose some challenges, but it was certainly a survivable event. By the way, in six years of driving to this bus stop, we never missed the bus.

You might protest that some negative outcomes are devastating, and no amount of "positive thinking" will gloss over that. I thoroughly agree. I'm not suggesting that you'll be happy if the bad thing happens. I'm only suggesting that a detached appraisal of the potential consequences might make your anxiety more manageable.

Another great question to ask is:

"Do I have any control or influence over what happens? If so, what practical steps can I take to increase the chances of a positive outcome?"

Severe anxiety can create a kind of behavioral paralysis. We could be taking constructive action, but we obsess, brood, and wallow in our misery instead. I have coached a number of graduate students who were struggling to complete their doctoral dissertations. It's not uncommon for these students to have negative thoughts such as, "My advisor will hate my draft. I won't pass my oral exam. I'll never finish my degree and get a job." Unfortunately, they become so fixated on those negative thoughts that they procrastinate on their work. Their inactivity might lead to the very negative consequence they fear, whereas constructive action would increase their chances for a positive outcome.

I'll have more to say about the relationship between negative thoughts, anxiety, and action in the next chapter.

Here's another good question to ask:

**"If the "bad event" happens,
how will I cope with it?"**

Sometimes we're so focused on possible negative outcomes that we forget that we are not helpless in dealing with their consequences. We may have skills, resources, talents, and supportive relationships that could see us through almost any troubling event. Most of us are more resilient than we realize.

Why do you make out a will or buy life insurance? It's not that you really expect to die in the next year. You just want to have a plan in case you do. Thinking about life insurance and wills may be uncomfortable, but it won't cause your death. Hopefully, having life insurance actually makes you less anxious because you know your loved ones will be cared for after you die.

Take this same approach to any "bad event" that you're dreading. If your boyfriend breaks up with you, how will you go about recovering from the loss? If you lose your job, how will you go about getting another one? If your teenage child fails in school, what steps will you take to address the situation?

For me, this simple step has often been a lifesaver. My first instinct is to think of the negative outcome and then spiral down into "catastrophe-thinking" such as, "That would be awful. I couldn't stand that." Obviously, that kind of thinking just makes me feel terrible and doesn't do anything to solve the problem.

But if I stop myself and say, "Yes, that would be very bad, and I certainly don't want it to happen. Nevertheless, if it did happen, how would I cope with it? What would I do to minimize the bad consequences? What could I do to even make some good come from it?"

I have worked with countless clients who were incredibly stressed out about their jobs. They had controlling bosses, vicious office politics, or unreasonable workloads. As unhappy as they were, they were terrified at the prospect of unemployment. Burdened with debt and having families to support, they saw themselves as having no choice but endure their current misery.

Here's what I often say to these clients, "I agree that it's probably best for you to do whatever you can to keep your job. Our work will focus on dealing with the controlling boss, rising above office politics, and finding ways to manage your heavy workload. Nevertheless, I think you also need an exit strategy. That is, you need to have a plan to figure out how you're going to cope if you lose your job."

If the client is agreeable to this, we get to work. I help him or her brainstorm alternative jobs, explore how to network, and possibly refer him or her to vocational testing. Sometimes, this process has gone so well, that the client has found a much more satisfying line of work. Some clients have stayed in their current job but were more relaxed because they knew they had options. Some clients decided they wanted to be let go because they were expecting a generous severance package. It's a lot of fun to have a client say, "I was laid off last week," and I can honestly say, "Congratulations!"

Finally, a last question to ask:

"If the bad thing happens, what will still be good in my life?"

I once worked with a client who was embroiled in a bitter divorce. His wife had hired a cutthroat attorney, and he was convinced that she was out to get every dime she could get. When we outlined his feared outcomes, he pictured himself losing his house, car, and most of his earthly goods. Although there really wasn't much chance of that, he couldn't stop thinking that he was headed for poverty.

Finally, one day he arrived for his session and said, "I've decided to stop worrying about the money. They can take every penny, but they can't devour me." That was certainly true. This man had a good education, an excellent work history, and many supportive family and friends. By "counting his blessings," he realized that he could survive even if his divorce turned out to be very unfavorable for him. As it turned out, he and his ex-wife were able to come to a fairly amicable agreement.

More Negative Thinking Habits

We have already discussed "negative mind reading" and "catastrophic thinking" as common thinking habits that lead to anxiety. Pioneers in CBT such as Aaron Beck have identified several more common mental habits that contribute to our emotional distress. Let's review a few of these.

All or none thinking: When we engage in "all or none thinking," things are either perfect or they're completely awful. If I don't get a 100 percent on the test then I failed miserably. If you don't like one thing about me, you hate everything about me. If I over-ate a little on Monday, then I might as well give up my diet for the rest of the week.

All or none thinking contributes to anxiety by making us feel that everything must turn out perfect. Anything less would be a catastrophe.

As always, the cure for this kind of thinking is to ask, "What are the real consequences if things don't turn out perfectly, and how will I cope with those consequences?"

So, let's look at the example of the less than perfect grade. If I say to myself, "OK, I made an 82, but I had hoped for better. Is an 82 really so terrible? What can I learn from this and how can I do better next time?"

Let's consider the example that someone doesn't like something about me. Does that mean they dislike everything about me? Even if they don't like me at all, can I live with that? I might not like it, but do I have to make myself miserable over someone else's opinion of me?

What about the example of not following my diet perfectly? Does that necessarily mean that I have completely blown it and should just give up?

Labeling: This is the unfortunate mental habit of calling ourselves (or other people) names if we are not pleased with how something turned out. Common negative labels include "stupid," "lazy," "failure," and so on.

Labeling contributes to anxiety by creating a sense of pressure and urgency that might not be warranted. Likewise, negative labels lessen our confidence in handling difficult or stressful events.

I often work with clients who are unsatisfied with their productivity and time management. These clients are often burdened by thoughts that they are "lazy" or "incompetent" or "a real loser." The sad thing is that these self-imposed labels rarely motivate them toward productive activity. Instead, the labels actually discourage them because they think, "I'm a lazy, incompetent loser. You can't expect much from me."

The cure for labeling is to realize that most labels actually are not of much use. No one acts "lazy" or "stupid" all the time, and everyone acts "lazy" or "stupid" some of the time. So, what defines a "lazy" person?

It makes more sense to evaluate ourselves (and others) by using more objective standards. For example, I might say, "I didn't get as much done today as I had hoped," or "I made a decision that I now regret."

People who suffer from anxiety often compound their misery by attaching negative labels to themselves. They might see themselves as "weak," or "crazy," If you do this to yourself, let me urge you to question your thinking. It's bad enough to be anxious. Why make it worse by calling yourself names?

Over-generalization: When we over-generalize, we assume that bad things that happened in the past are bound to happen in the future. Or, if things go wrong some of the time, they will go wrong every single time. The key words to look for are "always" and "never." "I always mess up." "I'll never get a job (promotion, date, etc.)." "Bad things always happen to me." "I never get a break!"

Over-generalization creates anxiety by shattering any sense of hope or optimism. For example, if I'm sure that I "always" embarrass myself when I speak in front of a group, I will never try. Likewise, if I believe that "no one will hire someone my age," I won't look for a job.

We battle over-generalization by seeing each event as separate from the others. Just because I have not found a job yet, it doesn't mean I will "never" find one. If I hadn't had success yet, I might need to change my approach or consider other job options, but it certainly isn't reason to give up.

Disqualifying the positive: Individuals who suffer from anxiety and depression tend to discount anything good that they do or anything good that happens to them. If they make a good grade, they'll protest, "It was an easy test." If you compliment them on a job well done, they'll say, "Anyone could do it."

Here's an extreme example. Doris was a young woman that I worked with years ago. One day when she arrived for her appointment, our receptionist casually complimented her on her outfit. As our therapy session was starting, she told me that she knew that I had told the receptionist to compliment her. When I told her that I had not told the receptionist any such thing, she refused to believe me. Her self-esteem was so low that she couldn't imagine that any compliment would be "real."

I often give anxious clients "homework" assignments in which they gradually confront feared situations. Very often, they discount their early success by insisting that they "got lucky" or that "anyone could have done that."

The antidote for discounting the positive is to allow yourself to take some genuine pleasure in your successes. It's perfectly OK to take some healthy pride in what you do well.

"Should" thoughts: Life's biggest challenges are to accept ourselves as we are, other people as they are, and the world as it is. We often berate ourselves with unnecessary guilt because we "should" ("ought to," "must," "have to") be different. We get angry with others because they "should" be different. We are frustrated with the world because it "should" be different.

"Should" thoughts contribute to anxiety by creating a sense of urgency and moral imperative to situations that might not really be that serious. For instance, if you focus on the thought, "I should be further along with my career," you might become paralyzed with guilt and fear. This would be especially true if your "should" thoughts were followed by, "I'm a failure" (all or none thinking, labeling), "I haven't accomplished anything" (overgeneralization, disqualifying the positive), and "I'll never succeed" (negative fortune telling).

My favorite way to overcome "should" thoughts is to soften them up a bit. I substitute "should," "must," "ought to," or "have to," with phrases such as "It would be nice," "I wish," or "I would prefer." Thus, I would substitute, "I should be further along with my career," with "It would be nice if I were further along with my career." This might seem like too subtle a difference to make any difference, but try it anyway. You will be surprised at how this slight change of wording can change the intensity of your feelings.

Mind reading: Later in Chapter Ten, we will explore the topic of Social Anxiety. We will see that most social anxiety arises from the unfortunate thinking habit of "mind reading." We are anxious around other people because we worry about what they think about us. Anxious individuals often assume that other people are thinking badly about them, even if there is little evidence to support this belief.

The antidote is to question your negative assumptions. Do you know for certain that they are thinking badly of you? Is it possible, that they're not concerned about you at all? Maybe they're worried about what you think about them.

We will learn a lot more about mind reading in the chapter on Social Anxiety.

"Talking Back" to Our Negative Thoughts

No one is immune to these negative thinking habits. We all use them. The fact that we recognize these habits in ourselves does not mean that we are stupid, crazy, or generally irrational people. However, these very same thinking habits are the source of much of our unhappiness.

As mentioned before, the key to getting better is to identify negative thoughts, discover how they might be distorted or irrational, and substitute our negative thoughts with more realistic, neutral, or positive thoughts. This is the Second C of Anxiety Recovery: Correct your thinking.

Let me share an example of how to "talk back" to your negative thoughts. I recently had the opportunity to speak to over 900 mental health professionals. As the time came near for the presentation, I started to get anxious. So, I took a few minutes to write down my automatic thoughts.

- "I'm going to mess up." (Fortune telling)
- "I've talked to groups before but never such a large one. Those groups were a lot easier." (Disqualifying the positive, fortune telling)
- "I'll make a fool of myself." (Labeling, fortune telling)
- "They won't like my presentation." (Mind reading)

Let's start with my thought, "They won't like my presentation." I "talked back" to this automatic thought by asking questions.

> Question: "Am I 100% certain that they won't like it?"
> Answer: "No, I have usually received good feedback for past presentations."
> Question: "Is there any evidence to suggest that this presentation would not also be well received?"
> Answer: "No, there's no evidence to suggest that they won't like it."
> Question: "Is there anything that I can do to increase the chances that they will like my presentation?"

Answer: "Yes, I can prepare very well and include lots of good examples."

So, based on my questions, I was able to develop a more rational alternative. "If I prepare well, there's a very good chance that most of the people in the audience will enjoy it."

I followed a similar procedure for each of the negative automatic thoughts. In no time at all, I was much more relaxed. By the way, the presentation was very well received.

Anti-anxiety Scripts

To further illustrate how to "talk back" to your anxious thoughts, here are a few case studies that illustrate the Second C: Correct your thinking. As always, client names and demographic information has been changed to protect confidentiality.

Steve was in his early 50's and was a senior sales representative for a firm that provided software for small and midsize companies. His company had recently been sold, and he was working under new management. Steve was very experienced in his field, but his new employers didn't seem to value his time-tested approach to building long-term relationships with customers. Instead, they were pushing for quick profits and gave him unreasonably high sales quotas. When he first came to see me, he was paralyzed with anxiety. He was constantly worried that he wouldn't meet his sales goals and would be fired.

Here's a summary of his anxiety-producing thoughts: "If I don't make my sales goals, I'll get fired. At my age, I'll never get another job that will pay anything close to what I make now. We'll lose everything! That would be more than I could stand."

Like many clients, Steve initially resisted the idea that his **thoughts** were part of the problem. He considered his thoughts to be a perfectly accurate reflection of the **reality** of his situation.

But let's look a little deeper. Is he doing any "fortune telling?" Yes, clearly he is predicting a number of "bad events" including not reaching his sales goals, getting fired, not finding another job, losing everything he owns, and not being able to "stand" the consequences.

Steve worked very hard at "talking back" to his anxious thoughts. Eventually he learned to ask himself the following questions:

- How likely was it that he would not reach his sales goals? Is there anything else that might happen?
- What are the real consequences of not reaching his sales goals?
- What can he do to increase the likelihood that he will reach his sales goals?
- What would be the real consequences of losing his job?
- How would he cope with losing his job?
- What would he still have left?

After honestly answering each of these questions, Steve was able to create a more accurate and less anxiety-provoking script.

"Yes, I'm having some trouble reaching my sales goals this year. I'm not sure if I'll reach them or not. I have made some good sales this quarter, so I have at least a 50-50 chance of reaching my goals. I'm not sure what the consequences of not reaching my goals would be. Perhaps I should have a heart-to-heart talk with my manager to see where I stand. I might lose my job, but I have a good record with the company, so it's more likely that I'll be put on a performance program. Although that would be embarrassing at this point in my career, it wouldn't kill me. And although it would certainly be a hardship if I lost my job, I would just have to work hard to find a new one as soon as I could. I've got some good job experiences that could help me find new employment. Maybe I should update my resume and do a little networking just in case."

The anti-anxiety script does not deny his problems. Yes, he is struggling to reach his sales goals. Yes, he might lose his job. Yes, losing his job would pose some major problems. But, notice how the new script takes a more neutral stance and focuses on problem-solving rather than catastrophic thinking. In time, Steve's anxiety was significantly reduced. Eventually, his employers recognized the value of his approach and adopted many of his ideas.

Kevin, 19, had been struggling with severe panic attacks for about five years. He often experienced intense anxiety whenever he was away from his family or in situations where he felt "trapped." For example, he was reluctant to go to movie theaters. Here were his anxiety-provoking thoughts: "I might have a panic attack and won't be able to get out of the theater. If the movie is boring, I'll start thinking about having a panic attack. If I had a panic attack in the theater, I would be so embarrassed that I couldn't stand it."

Kevin learned to "talk back" to his scary thoughts by asking the following questions. "How likely is it that I'll have a panic attack in the theater?" "If I have one, how will I deal with it?" "If the movie is boring, how will I deal with that?" "If it were really important for me to get out of the theater, what would I do?"

Kevin created the following anti-anxiety script:

> "I have learned how to cope with panic attacks. I can use my deep breathing techniques and ride it out. Although panic attacks are uncomfortable, I now understand that they are not harmful or dangerous. I have been in boring movies before. If I absolutely feel that I must leave the theater, I can do so. People leave theaters all the time. It's not such a bad thing to do."

Like most clients, Kevin had to repeat this process several times before he finally "got it." After a couple of months, Kevin had experienced a remarkable transformation. In the past, he had been virtually disabled by worry and chronic panic attacks. By the end of treatment, he was a happy and outgoing young man.

Considering the Source

Many clients find it difficult to dispute their negative thoughts. One of the hardest things to accept is the idea that thoughts are just thoughts and do not necessarily represent reality. The thoughts certainly **feel** real.

To help clients with this, I have adapted a technique described by Dr. Tamar Chansky in her treatment of obsessive-compulsive disorder in children.

Here's how it works. Once you have identified and written down your anxiety-provoking thoughts, *imagine that someone you disrespect* is saying these negative things to you.

Rather than seeing these ideas as coming from your own mind, imagine someone for whom you have little regard is saying these things to you. Many of my clients have great fun with this idea. Often, they choose characters from TV shows or movies such as Archie Bunker of "All in the Family," Biff from "Back to the Future," and Cousin Eddie from "National Lampoon's Vacation." Certain celebrities have also been picked such as Paris Hilton and Howard Stern. Since they have almost no regard for this person, they find it easy to dispute and disregard what they say.

Charles was a gifted commercial designer. However, he had great difficulty focusing on his work because he was constantly worried that his work would be viciously criticized and rejected. In truth, his work was usually well received, and his clients were usually satisfied. Nevertheless, he was plagued by thoughts such as, "Your clients will hate this work. You must create a perfect work or else it will be useless junk."

In challenging these negative thoughts, Charles imagined Archie Bunker as his critic. This made it easy for him to respond with statements such as, "Poor Archie, you have no idea what you're talking about. Go ahead and babble on. I'm not going to pay any attention to you."

Action step: Once you have identified your anxiety-provoking thoughts, imagine that someone for whom you have little respect is speaking them. How would you respond if such a person were saying these negative things?

Core Beliefs

Are you able to see the relationship between your thoughts and anxiety? Are you having any success in "talking back" to some of your anxiety-producing thoughts? If not, perhaps your "core beliefs" are getting in the way.

As the name suggests, a "core belief" is a deeply-held attitude or "hidden assumption." Although our core beliefs largely govern our feelings and behavior, we are usually not aware of them. We have to dig down deep into our own thought patterns in order to discover them.

My anxious clients have taught me a lot about the importance of core belief. Many times I would jump right into employing CBT techniques and then be frustrated that we weren't making any progress. More often than not, there was a pesky core belief in the way. We had to examine that core belief before we could make any progress.

Everyone is different, but there are certain themes that run through many unhealthy and self-defeating core beliefs. Here is a list of common dysfunctional core beliefs. Each will have a small element of truth, but will be largely untrue and extremely unhelpful. After each core belief, I will share some information that should help refute them.

"My anxiety is completely caused by a chemical imbalance in my brain. Non-medical treatment will not work. I must rely on my medicine alone to feel OK."

Yes, there is a physical component of anxiety. However, that doesn't mean that medicine is the only treatment. There is considerable evidence that cognitive-behavioral therapy is as effective as medication if not more so.

"My anxiety is a moral weakness. If I had more faith, I wouldn't be anxious. I probably deserve to feel bad."

Overcoming anxiety is a skill like playing the piano, driving, typing, or learning a foreign language. You're not weak or lacking in faith if you haven't learned how to do these things yet.

"I have had such a troubled life that I am destined to be anxious. I have suffered too much trauma to ever hope to recover from my anxiety."

Yes, our past difficulties may have left us feeling hopeless, discouraged, or inadequate. But, these feelings themselves are the result of how we are thinking **in the present**. Dealing with our current thoughts, feelings, and behaviors is the key to recovery. Many people who have experienced horrendous abuse or neglect have found recovery through learning to live in the here and now.

"I mustn't feel any anxiety at all. Even a little anxiety is bound to explode into extreme anxiety. I cannot tolerate even the slightest discomfort."

The goal of treatment is not the complete elimination of all anxiety. A certain amount of anxiety is a normal and expected part of life. Low levels of anxiety can even help increase focus and motivation. In fact, a low level of anxiety can actually be a good thing. Whenever we take on a new challenge, we are bound to experience some anxiety. Anxiety is a sign that we are growing. A low level of anxiety doesn't have to explode into severe anxiety.

"No one in my family understands how I'm suffering. I can't get over my anxiety until I get them to understand and have empathy for my problems."

It is true that no one else can truly understand the nature of *our* suffering. It is always desirable and helpful if our family understands and supports us, but it is not an essential aspect of recovery. Often our family members have their own problems and concerns. Often their intentions are good, but they don't know how to help us. Even when their intentions are not good, they don't have control over how we cope with our problems.

Did you see yourself in any of those core beliefs? Perhaps you saw a little of yourself in several of them. If so, I invite you to create your own new, healthier core belief. You don't have to be overly optimistic but just write out a core belief that you can endorse. Even if you can't fully believe it now, write out what you would **like** to believe. What kind of belief would be the most helpful for you right now?

It's important that you develop this core belief for yourself. However, to help you along, I have written out a model core belief for you to use. Feel free to modify as it suits you.

"Because I want the benefits of overcoming my anxiety, I choose to believe that the principles of CBT might be helpful. Although I'm not sure that they'll work, I'm willing to try them out. I'm willing to make the effort to learn and apply these principles."

You'll notice that this model core belief is not "positive thinking." In fact, it's rather neutral. If you are comfortable with developing a more positive-sounding core belief, then do so. But, you're not required to have a "positive attitude" for these principles to work. A "less negative attitude" will be enough for now.

The next action step is for you to develop your new, more helpful core belief. Write it out and review it regularly.

Summarizing What We've Learned So Far

Calm your body: We have learned the physical symptoms of anxiety are uncomfortable but are not harmful or dangerous. We have also learned how to reduce or eliminate the physical symptoms through deep breathing, relaxation exercise and visualization.

Correct your thinking: We have also explored the cognitive side of anxiety. We have seen how our own negative thought patterns are the basis of our anxiety. We have learned how to identify and correct our distorted thinking.

In the next chapter, we will review the third component of anxiety: the behavioral. We will learn the Third C of anxiety recovery: Confront your fears.

Chapter Six

THE THIRD C OF ANXIETY RECOVERY

CONFRONT YOUR FEARS

The third and perhaps most destructive aspect of anxiety is the behavioral side. It is sad to see how people allow their fears to control their behavior and thus control their lives.

The behavioral aspect of anxiety is simply stated. Because anxiety feels uncomfortable, people tend to avoid situations that make them anxious. If driving on the freeway makes you anxious, you will avoid freeway driving. If you suffer from social anxiety, you'll avoid meetings and parties. If you tend to have panic attacks in the shopping mall, you won't go shopping.

Avoiding these situations may seem like a very reasonable thing to do. However, avoidance only makes anxiety worse. The more we avoid fear-provoking situations, the greater the fear will become.

It is crucial that you understand this key point. Avoidance only makes anxiety worse. To get over anxiety, you must somehow do the thing you're afraid to do. This is the Third C of Anxiety Recovery: Confront your fears.

Here's a well-known experiment with laboratory mice. The experimenter constructs a "mouse house" with two compartments. One compartment is white and the other is black with a doorway connecting the two. The floor of the black compartment has an electric grid through which the mouse can be administered a mildly painful but not harmful electric shock.

The mouse is placed in the black compartment and is immediately shocked. The mouse reacts by randomly jumping and running around. Just by chance, it goes through the door and into the white compartment where there is no shock.

At this point, the electricity is disconnected and the mouse is never shocked again. The experimenter places him back in the black compartment. What do you think the mouse does? He immediately runs into the white compartment. If you pick him up and place him back in the black compartment, he will immediately run into the white. In fact, he will continue this pattern every time he is placed in the black.

Why does he do this? It's basically the result of simple conditioning. The mouse associates the black compartment with the shock and the resulting pain and fear. Every time he runs into the white compartment, he is rewarded by the reduction in his fear. This pattern of avoidance quickly becomes a learned habit.

If the mouse is placed in the black compartment with no way to escape, it will initially respond with great fear. However, in time, the mouse will "get use to" the black compartment and will not be afraid.

That is due to the process of habituation. This refers to the tendency of an organism to adapt to its surroundings. Stimuli that initially evoke a strong response will eventually lose the ability to trigger such a strong response.

As a teen, I saw the Alfred Hitchcock thriller, "Psycho." Who can forget that shower scene and how much it scared us the first time we saw it? However, I have probably watched that scene a hundred times since then, and it's long since lost the ability to freak me out.

Exposure

The mouse adapting to the black compartment and my repeated viewings of "Psycho" illustrate the same process, exposure. One of the best ways to overcome anxiety is to purposely "expose" ourselves to those very situations that make us anxious.

Exposure can be carried out in a variety of ways. One method is "gradual exposure." As the name suggests, you place yourself in the fearful situation but not all at once. You do it in manageable steps.

Clark had a history of panic attacks whenever he ventured away from his home or his car. He only felt safe when he knew that he could easily return to his home. Because of his fear, he avoided concerts, movies, large social gatherings, and public transportation such as busses or subways. Clark's treatment helped him begin with situations that were only mildly anxiety provoking. He started by taking a few weekend trips on the local rapid rail system. Since it was the weekend, he didn't have to deal with large crowds. He began by only riding from one station to the next. Then he would ride the train for two stops. Then he rode for two stops and walked around a shopping mall for 15 minutes before returning to his car. Eventually, he was able to travel all over town and attend many events that he previously had avoided.

Another way to do gradual exposure is to have someone with you when you first place yourself in the feared situation. If you have social anxiety, first attend a party with a friend before venturing to a social gathering by yourself. If you are trying to overcome your fear of freeway driving, first do some driving with a trusted friend in the car.

Gradual exposure can even be accomplished by just **imagining** the feared situation. With clients with social anxiety, I sometimes have them imagine attending a social event or speaking in front of a group. For obvious reasons, clients who are afraid to drive on the freeway are often the most reluctant to tackle that fear head on. For them, it's often helpful to have them first imagine driving on the freeway and then driving with someone else in the car.

Such a gradual approach is often helpful but not always necessary. You might decide to try sudden exposure or "flooding." That is, you place yourself in the most anxiety-provoking situation without approaching it in gradual steps.

Dr. David Burns, one of the pioneers of CBT, describes a situation in high school where he practiced sudden exposure. David wanted to be a crew member for the school's drama production. His first task was to climb a tall stepladder in order to work on the lights above the stage. David protested that he was afraid of heights, but the teacher had no sympathy. The teacher gave him these instructions, "Climb up to the top of the ladder. You'll feel scared. Stay there until you're not scared anymore." That's exactly what David did. At first he was terrified, but he eventually "habituated" to the height and was not scared at all.

The drama instructor was not a therapist, but he certainly applied just the right principles of CBT in this case.

Do What You're Afraid to Do: Do it Quickly!

Do you remember having to give oral book reports in school? When I was in middle school, it seemed as though every teacher felt obliged to assign them. I hated them! I sat through many a class, terrified that I would be called on. If I wasn't called on the first day, I might get a day's reprieve, but it would only ruin my night as I knew that I would probably have to do it the next day.

Finally, I got smart and started volunteering to give my report first. Yes, I was terrified, but once the report was over, I could sit, relax, and watch my classmates suffer.

This illustrates an important truth. *Often, "thinking" about something is much worse than "doing" it.* Often, the best antidote for anxiety is take action. Do the thing you're scared to do, and in time it won't scare you anymore. Also, the sooner you take action, the sooner your anxiety will go away!

I try to apply this principle on a daily basis. If I have something on my "to do" list that makes me anxious, I will usually do it first.

For example, let's say that I have a number of phone calls to make, and I anticipate that one of the calls might involve some conflict or confrontation. Even though my impulse will be to put that call off, I push myself to make it first.

Burt was a salesman whose livelihood depended on marketing phone calls. Since he told himself, "I'm just bothering these people. They won't want my product," he was quite anxious making these calls, which led him to start putting them off. He would clear his desk, read his mail, and do anything to put off the phone calls. His treatment involved coaching him to make his calls first and then reward himself by engaging in more pleasant activities.

Embracing Anxiety

Since so much of this book is devoted to attacking and overcoming anxiety, it might seem strange for me to talk about "embracing" anxiety. There's a wonderful paradox at work here. One of the best ways to overcome severe anxiety problems is to allow yourself, even encourage yourself, to experience moderate levels of anxiety.

In Chapter Three, I mentioned that many people are afraid of their anxieties. The feeling of anxiety is so uncomfortable and their thoughts are so negative and catastrophic that they believe they must avoid all anxiety-provoking situations at all cost.

If we could record their thoughts ("core beliefs") about anxiety, they would be something like, "The feeling of anxiety means that something terrible is happening to me. Anxiety is so uncomfortable, and I am so inadequate in dealing with it, that I must avoid any situation that makes me anxious. If something makes me anxious, I must not do it."

Obviously, someone with these core beliefs will avoid any situation that poses any risks. They will let their fears control their lives and thus possibly miss out on many of life's blessings. This is such a shame!

I encourage my clients to develop a new and quite different "core belief" about anxiety. Together, we talk about situations in which they tried something new. They started school, learned to drive, moved to a new community, started a new job, or got married and raised children. As we review these events, clients usually remember that they were anxious every time. However, as they "habituated" to their new situation, they became much less anxious.

The clear point here is that all human growth and progress involves getting out of our comfort zones and experiencing some level of anxiety. Seen this way, anxiety is actually a good thing. It means we're growing and stretching ourselves to accomplish something new.

Whenever I take on any new project, I always experience some anxiety. As I work through my anxiety, I exercise my "emotional muscles," which ultimately makes me stronger and more self-confident.

A more helpful "core belief" about anxiety would be,

"I'm trying something new and different, so I am having some normal feelings of anxiety. My anxiety is actually a good thing in that it means that I am growing. I have productive ways to deal with my anxiety, so it won't become unmanageable."

I encourage you to adopt a similar "core belief" and learn to embrace rather than fearfully avoid anything that might trigger anxious thoughts and feelings.

The Key Elements of All Anxiety Recovery: The Three C's.

Now that we have reviewed the three components of anxiety, we will apply what we've learned to attack specific anxiety problems. Although the specific techniques vary from one anxiety problem to another, all good treatment for anxiety problems contains the following three elements:

1. Calm your body: We deal with the physical symptoms of anxiety by learning to re-label them as benign and reducing them via breathing and other techniques.

2. Correct your thinking: We identify how our negative thoughts are making us anxious and how to replace anxiety-provoking thoughts with more neutral or positive thoughts.

3. Confront your fears: We stop avoiding situations that make us anxious. Instead, we expose ourselves to these situations and do the very things that make us anxious. This includes learning to embrace some low or moderate levels of anxiety when taking on new challenges.

We will now discuss a number of anxiety problems. We will begin with one of the most dramatic and yet misunderstood: panic attacks.

Chapter Seven
PANIC ATTACKS

There are few experiences more frightening than a panic attack. This is particularly true if it's your first one. I have seen confident, self-assured executives become completely incapacitated by panic attacks. I have seen outgoing, active individuals become so worried about their panic attacks that they were reluctant to leave home.

Panic attacks do not discriminate in regard to age, race, sex, or economic status. Martin was a high-powered executive. His first attack was triggered by an episode of indigestion caused by a big seafood dinner. He was extremely frightened by this episode, which in turn triggered more attacks. When I saw him, he had already been to the emergency room twice. Martin was a very well adjusted man who prided himself on his composure and self-control. He couldn't imagine why he was having these attacks. His family life was good, his job was good, and he was leading a very happy and purposeful life. However, his attacks had him completely humbled, and he was desperate for help. Fortunately, CBT worked very well for him.

Allison was a teacher. She experienced her first attack in the classroom. On two separate occasions, the paramedics were called and Allison was taken to the ER. Of course, she found this humiliating. What did her students and colleagues think of this? "They must think I'm a loony." Well, she wasn't a "loony," and she responded very well to CBT and is no longer bothered by panic attacks at all

What is a panic attack? According to the Diagnostic and Statistical Manual (DSM-IV), of the American Psychiatric

Association, a panic attack is "A discrete period of intense fear or discomfort that is accompanied by at least 4 of the following 13 somatic or cognitive symptoms."

1. Palpitations, pounding heart, or accelerated heart rate
2. Sweating
3. Trembling or shaking
4. Sensations of shortness of breath or smothering
5. Feeling of choking
6. Chest pain or discomfort
7. Nausea or abdominal distress
8. Feeling dizzy, unsteady, lightheaded, or faint
9. Derealization (feelings of unreality) or depersonalization (being detached from oneself)
10. Fear of losing control or going crazy
11. Fear of dying
12. Numbness or tingling sensations
13. Chills or hot flashes

Panic attacks usually occur suddenly and build to a peak within 10 minutes or less. The person may experience "an imminent sense of danger or doom and an urge to escape." Although 4 of the 13 symptoms must be present for the event to be diagnosed as a panic attack, some individuals experience panic-like or limited-symptom attacks, which may involve only one symptom. For example, an individual might fear excessive perspiration in social situations or a sudden attack of diarrhea.

As noted above, a panic attack usually occurs suddenly and reaches a peak within 10 minutes or less. Some of my clients have reported attacks lasting hours or more. However, upon further questioning, it usually turns out that they were experiencing a series of attacks as their anxiety would wax and wane over an extended period of time.

Some panic attacks occur "out of the blue" in that they are not connected to any particular situation. Other panic attacks are clearly associated with certain situations.

Many of my clients have told me that their first panic attacks were the most frightening and distressing experiences of their lives. Many believed they were having a heart attack or other medical problem, so they were taken to the emergency room. Even after being checked out medically, many continued to believe that they had some undiagnosed medical problem.

After the first panic attack, many individuals worry about the possibility of another attack. They might constantly monitor themselves for any signs of an attack. Of course, this watchfulness makes them more sensitive to even normal physical arousal, which in turn increases the likelihood of another attack.

Many people worry about the implications of the attacks. They become demoralized and their self-esteem suffers. They wrongly believe that they are losing control of their mental faculties or that they are somehow weak or lacking in character. Individuals with strong religious beliefs may berate themselves for what they see as a lack of faith. It's not uncommon for the individual to develop serious depression as a consequence of their panic attacks. As we will see later, these responses are an unfortunate result of lack of knowledge about what a panic attack really is.

After the first attack, some individuals begin to fear certain situations in which they anticipate that an attack might occur. This might include any situation in which escape might be impossible, difficult, or embarrassing, or they perceive that a panic attack would be dangerous. Thus, they might avoid being alone either at home or away from home. They might avoid certain modes of transportation such as busses, trains or airplanes. They might avoid driving on freeways where it would be difficult to stop or get off the road if they had an attack. They might avoid crowds, meetings, or any social situation in which it would be difficult to escape.

This pattern of avoiding certain situations is called Agoraphobia. Technically, the term means, "fear of the market place." Yet, it's not so much the "place" that the person fears—it's the fear of having a panic attack in that place.

As you can imagine, once the person begins avoiding situations, it seriously disrupts his or her life. I once worked with a young man who had only experienced two panic attacks. However, these experiences were so upsetting, and he so feared future attacks that he greatly limited his activity. He essentially went from home to work to home. He didn't venture far from his home. He wouldn't go to malls or other crowded places, and he would not ride on public transportation. However, at least he could go to work and make it to his therapy sessions. Some individuals are so paralyzed with fear that they will not venture away from their home—especially not on their own.

Common Misconceptions about Panic Attacks

Some people have inaccurate ideas of what panic attacks are and what causes them. This is unfortunate because it prevents people from getting the help they need.

Wrong idea number one: "Since panic attacks are largely physical reactions, they can only be treated by medication. The only way to stop panic attacks is to find the right drug."

Yes, there are very distressing physical symptoms in a panic attack. Yes, sometimes medications can be helpful, especially if the symptoms are severe or if the person is also depressed. Sometimes medication helps ease anxiety just enough to make it easier for the patient to participate in CBT.

However, relying purely on medical interventions does not help the individual understand what is going on and to develop the coping skills necessary to overcome attacks. The person may experience some much-needed relief, but he/she is not empowered to cope with attacks.

Here is the second common misconception, "Panic attacks are a sign of a deep-seated psychological problem that can only be treated with insight-oriented psychotherapy."

Early in my career, I had the same misconception. When clients came for help with their panic attacks, I immediately started looking for "deeper" causes. Were they struggling with a current life issue? Were there inner conflicts that they needed to face? Sometimes this approach was helpful, but more often than not, the clients left in frustration. Their primary need was to be rid of their panic attacks—not an in-depth exploration of their deeper needs and motives.

Certainly, panic attacks often occur in the context of other problems. There may be excessive work stress, marital conflicts, family problems, or unresolved childhood issues. However, I have found it usually best to directly treat the panic attacks first. Once clients are confident that they can overcome the panic attacks, they are often ready to explore other areas of concern.

What Causes Panic Attacks?

Remember how I "unpacked" anxiety. I divided anxiety into its three component parts: 1. Physical, 2. Cognitive, 3. Behavioral. Effective treatment for panic attacks addresses all three components and makes use of the Three C's of Anxiety Recovery.

Let's begin with the physical side of panic. As mentioned in Chapter Four, the human body has an emergency response system that helps us flee when we are in a life-threatening situation. Running away requires a rapidly beating heart, fast breathing, tense muscles, blood flowing away from the skin and head, and interrupted digestion—all of the physical sensations usually associated with fear. All of these physical symptoms would save your life if you were really in danger, but they are of no use most of the time.

Simply stated, a panic attack occurs when the body has made a mistake. The emergency response system has been triggered when it isn't needed. Again, as was mentioned in Chapter Four, these reactions are uncomfortable, but they are not harmful or dangerous. These responses will also be time-limited and will go away in a short while. Also, these responses are much like what happens in the body when we are excited, angry, or engaging in physical exercise.

We don't know why the emergency response system is triggered this way. Some people are genetically predisposed to these reactions. Sometimes, the individual is going through a stressful period, which makes the body more susceptible to these responses. No matter how it gets started, it helps to consider what is happening as a mistake that will soon pass.

The cognitive component of panic follows the physical. When the emergency response system is triggered, the mind begins to search for answers. What is the danger? Since there is no obvious external danger, the mind assumes, "There must be something terribly wrong inside!" That is when the catastrophic thoughts occur—"I'm going crazy. I'm losing control. I'm cracking up. I'm having a heart attack. I'm dying. I have got to get out of here!"

Obviously, these scary thoughts only serve to increase the intensity of the body's emergency reaction. These increased physical sensations trigger more scary thoughts, which in turn trigger more physical sensations. So a vicious cycle develops with every-increasing panic.

Once someone has had their first panic attack, they are constantly on guard for the next one. This hyper-alertness only serves to increase the likelihood that another attack will be triggered.

The behavioral aspect of panic refers to the fact that people will often start avoiding any situation in which an attack might be particularly embarrassing or dangerous. So the person might start avoiding freeway driving, public transportation, shopping malls or large crowds.

In summary, here is the sequence of events in a panic attack:

1. The emergency response system is triggered in a situation in which there is no real danger. This reaction may occur because of some perceived threat or possibly as a result of a high level of chronic stress.

2. The conscious mind notices the physical arousal and starts looking for danger. Seeing no danger, the mind begins to generate exaggerated and unrealistic thoughts about the source of the "danger." These thoughts might include, "I'm having a heart attack. I'm dying. I'm going crazy. I've got to get out of

here. Something terrible is happening to me." Although these thoughts are completely false, they are perceived as true.

3. These thoughts in turn trigger even higher levels of physical arousal, thus triggering even more scary thoughts.

4. Eventually the attack goes away. Unfortunately, having had the first attack, the person is constantly worried about having another one. He/she begins to believe that he/she has some serious medical or psychological problem.

5. This makes him/her on guard for any situation in which an attack might occur. This anxious anticipation just increases the likelihood that another attack will happen. It becomes a self-fulfilling prophecy.

6. The person becomes particularly concerned about any situation in which he/she thinks that an attack would be dangerous or embarrassing. This includes enclosed areas where escape would be difficult if not impossible. This might include traveling on limited access highways, crossing bridges, traveling on public transportation or even sitting in the middle of a row of seats in a theater or lecture hall. It might include being alone where the person fears that they could get no medical help if an attack should occur. It might include social environments where an attack would be embarrassing. This is the condition referred to as Agoraphobia.

7. So, a pattern of avoidance is established. But since avoidance only serves to increase anxiety, the problem only gets worse.

Overcoming Panic Attacks

The overall strategy for overcoming panic attacks involves making use of the Three C's. You learn to calm your body, correct your thinking, and confront your fears. Here's a brief summary of how it works:

1. You learn how to re-label your physical arousal. Rather than perceiving it as a sign of danger, you remind yourself that it is an unpleasant but harmless feeling not unlike a minor headache, muscle ache, or indigestion. You remind yourself that it will pass. (Correct your thinking)

2. You do not fight the physical arousal. Instead, you ride it out. (Correct your thinking, Calm your body)

3. You use deep abdominal breathing and visualization techniques to reduce the intensity of the arousal until it passes.(Calm your body)

4. You have previously identified your frightening thoughts during an attack. You have identified and memorized more rational and realistic thoughts when you begin to have an attack. For example, instead of "This is horrible, I can't stand this," you say to yourself, "This is uncomfortable, but I know how to ride this out now." (Correct your thinking)
5. You do your best not to leave the situation in which the attack occurs. Instead, you endure the discomfort until it goes away on its own. (Confront your fears)

6. When you are having trouble refuting your frightening thoughts, "test" them by using the "experimental method." (Correct your thinking, confront your fears)

Experimental Method

Remember that a key element for overcoming panic attacks is the ability to challenge distorted or unrealistic thoughts such as "I'm dying," or "I'm losing control." Often just reminding yourself of the more realistic alternative is enough to diminish the attack. However, sometimes no amount of logic or reason will convince you that you aren't dying or losing control. So, when logic fails you, try the experimental method.

In the "experimental method," you actually "test" the validity of your irrational thoughts in an effort to prove them wrong. For example, if your scary thought is, "I'm losing control," you test this thought, by asking yourself, "If I were losing control, would I be able to remember the names of my children? Would I be able to alternatively raise and lower my right and left arm?" Then you "experiment." "Can I remember the names of my children? I can, so I must not be losing control." "Can I raise and lower my hands? I can, so I must not be losing control."

If your irrational thought is, "I'm dying," you ask yourself, "If I were dying, would I be able to do some jumping jacks?" Then, do some jumping jacks to convince yourself that you're not dying. Obviously, you need to have planned these experiments in advance, so you're ready to perform them when an attack occurs.

If you attend a workshop given by Dr. David Burns, he will often show a very moving video about a young woman client who had been paralyzed by panic attacks for many years. Dr. Burns convinces her to try to have an attack right there in his office. Sure enough, she begins to become extremely afraid.

She tells him that she just "knows" she is having a heart attack. He asks her, "If you were having a heart attack, could you stand." Slowly she stands up. He then asks, "If you were having a heart attack, could you do jumping jacks?" She is hesitant at first, but then she starts doing jumping jacks. As it turns out, this young woman works in a hospital and often sees cardiac patients. Dr. Burns asks her, "Is this what the heart attack patients do in your hospital? Do they stand next to their gurneys and do jumping jacks?" With this, the young woman burst into laughter. In an instant, she has had an amazing breakthrough. She now "knows" at a very deep level, that her fears were unwarranted. Dr. Burns reports that she had a few minor attacks after that time, but shortly thereafter all attacks stopped and she has been free of attacks for many years.

Tips for Overcoming Attacks

Experts agree that there are a number of excellent strategies that are very helpful in dealing with a panic attack in progress. Here are a few of them:

1. When the physical sensations are noticed, quickly remind yourself that they are harmless and that they will soon pass. Attack frightening thoughts with statements such as "I don't like the way I feel, but nothing bad is happening." "There is no tiger here!" "These feelings will pass; I can ride them out." "This is a lot like being excited, angry or exercising."

2. Remind yourself that you are safe and that there is no need to escape the situation that you are in. Hang in there.

3. Rather than fighting the attack, ride it out. Imagine that you are a surfer, and you're riding a wave into shore.

4. Practice deep abdominal breathing at times when you're already calm. Experience how it helps you feel even more relaxed. Then, when you sense the onset of a panic attack, you can use the breathing to help you get through it.

5. Take your attention away from your uncomfortable sensations by focusing on something else. Engage in something that occupies your mind such as silently reciting the multiplication tables or remembering the names of recent Presidents.

6. Focus your attention on some aspect of your physical environment. Count the ceiling tiles or windows; notice the patterns on the carpet or wallpaper, or notice all the different colors you see. Pay attention to any sounds.

7. If there are other people nearby, engage them in conversation. That will help take your attention away from your uncomfortable physical sensations.

8. If possible, do some sort of physical exercise. Start jogging or doing jumping jacks. Your body is preparing for motion, so move it. However, don't actually leave the situation you are in.

9. Calm yourself by visualizing pleasant scenes. Picture yourself at the beach. Remember a particularly happy time in your life and imagine that you are reliving the experience.

10. If you must temporarily retreat from the situation, you may do so. However, if at all possible, make yourself return to it as soon as you can. You want to break that pattern of avoidance that tends to perpetuate panic attacks.

11. Learn to not fear your body by intentionally creating some of the physical symptoms typical of panic. Make your heart rate increase by doing exercises, create a feeling of dizziness by spinning around, or create a sense of needing more air by breathing through a straw.

12. Use the experimental method to test and challenge frightening thoughts. "If I was losing control, would I be able to...?"

The primary purpose of all of these activities is to increase your confidence in your ability to handle a panic attack should it occur. In fact, you actually hope to create a small attack, so you can practice these skills.

Once your confidence has increased, you will no longer need to avoid situations that have triggered attacks in the past. In fact you will look forward to these situations. This, in turn, will greatly reduce the likelihood that a panic attack will occur.

These techniques work! Many of my clients who were plagued by intense and repeated attacks are now completely symptom free. If you do not feel that you can practice these techniques on your own, any good therapist who practices CBT can help you use them.

Now that we have discussed panic attacks and how to overcome them, let's examine two situations in which panic attacks pose particular problems: fear of flying and fear of driving on the freeway.

Chapter Eight
FEAR OF FLYING

I have worked with countless clients who were deathly afraid of flying. However, most people who are afraid of flying don't seek treatment. They just don't fly. Professional football commentator, John Madden, is very open about his long-standing fear of flying. Now, John Madden is a very tough guy, but he cannot bring himself to get on an airplane. Instead, he has a custom-made motor coach that takes him from one announcing assignment to another.

Many people, like John Madden, get by without ever flying. However, in doing so, they miss out on many wonderful travel opportunities. In addition, travel is an integral part of American business. I have known several people who passed up great promotions because the better job required travel. This is unfortunate because the principles of CBT are usually very effective in overcoming the fear of flying.

We all understand that there is some risk in flying. Although we know the statistics showing that flying in a commercial airliner is safer than driving in our car, we also know that a plane crash usually has deadly consequences.

However, the fear of crashing seems to play a relatively small part in most flying phobias. Instead, the main concern seems to be the fear of having a panic attack. That may surprise you, but I have certainly found that to be the case in my practice.

Let's review what we have learned about a panic attack in order to help us understand this. Remember, people who have had panic attacks begin to fear, and thus avoid any situation in which they cannot "get out." When you enter the cabin of an airliner, you are entering a relatively small, cylindrically shaped "tube." It's often crowded and you know that you will not be able to leave for the duration of the flight. What a perfect setting to brew up a panic attack. Add in the normal safety concerns and perhaps a little turbulence and you have the perfect ingredients for an attack.

When I ask my clients to verbalize their fears about flying, they usually do not focus on the potential for a crash. Instead, they worry about how they will feel or what they might do. Their "fortune-telling" will include thoughts like, "I'll crack up. I won't be able to stand it. I'll lose control. I'll go crazy. I'll want to get out. I'll freak out. I won't be able to breathe. There won't be enough air. I'll pass out. I'll make a fool of myself." These are all classic symptoms of panic attacks.

So if you learn how to cope with panic attacks, you will be well on your way to overcoming the fear of flying.

Brian had recently earned his Ph.D. Originally from the Midwest, he had found a great job in Atlanta. Brian had experienced a few panic episodes on flights, so he had long avoided traveling by air. When he consulted me, Brian found himself in a terrible jam. The holidays were coming, and he had accepted an invitation to visit his girlfriend's family in New York. Then, the commencement ceremonies for his doctorate were to be held at his school in Texas in early December. His girlfriend, her parents, and other relatives were all looking forward to that special day. Finally, he hoped to take his girlfriend to meet his parents in Iowa over Christmas. Obviously, the distances were too long and the available time too limited for him to drive to all of these places. So, Brian faced the daunting prospect of six flights in less than a month. Needless to say, he was terrified.

To make matters worse, Brian had been so afraid to face this issue that he had put off getting help. It was now early October, so we had about a month and a half to get him ready for the first flight. Brian was very doubtful that he could ever overcome his fears. Even though he would lose thousands of dollars in prepaid fares, he was seriously considering bailing out of the whole trip.

Obviously, we had a lot to do in a short period of time. First, we had to focus on his motivation. Why did he want to overcome his fear? He had a ton of reasons. He really wanted to share Thanksgiving with his girlfriend and her parents. He didn't want to let her down or offend her parents. He was excited about his commencement exercises. He had worked very hard for his degree and he wanted to celebrate. Finally, he always loved Christmas with his family, and he wanted his girlfriend to share the experience. With all this to gain, Brian decided he was willing to push himself a little.

Then, Brian and I addressed the physical aspect of panic. I taught him deep abdominal breathing, and he agreed to practice it regularly. Since he practiced it when he was already calm, he found that it came in handy during any stressful situation. When about to give a presentation at work, he took a few deep breaths to help him calm down and get centered. When he was stuck in rush hour traffic, he found that deep breathing helped him relax and be patient. He gained confidence in this technique, but he was still doubtful that it would help him endure a plane flight.

We then moved on to progressive relaxation and visualization. He learned how to relax his body while he pictured himself walking on a beach, looking at a beautiful sunset. We made a recording of this exercise and he listened to it regularly. He hoped to listen to his relaxation tape on the plane, but he was concerned that he would not be permitted to use his recording device. To prepare for this, he learned how to trigger his relaxed state by merely saying the word, "relax."

We then proceeded to cognitive interventions to correct his thinking. What were his catastrophic thoughts? He imagined that he would "crack up" and "freak out." I asked him to describe for me exactly what "crack up" would mean. He found it difficult to describe, except that he would feel very uncomfortable. So, I asked him, "If you feel uncomfortable, how will you cope with this?" We came up with an action plan. He would use his breathing, listen to his relaxation tape, and remind himself that he was safe and secure on the plane.

Brian had another very common catastrophic thought, "I won't be able to get out!" So, I asked him this question, "You'll be flying at over 30,000 feet. Under what circumstances would you ever want to get out?" Most clients feel very relieved to recognize the absurdity of their fearful thoughts.

We continued to do this for every negative thought. We would see where it was illogical and then substitute a more realistic thought.

"I'll crack up," was replaced with, "I might feel quite uncomfortable, but there is no reason to think that I'll lose my mental capacities."

"I won't be able to get out," was replaced with, "I am safe inside the plane. I have no need or desire to get out."

"I won't be able to breathe," was replaced with, "There is plenty of air on the plane. All I have to do is take a few deep abdominal breaths. That will prove that I can breathe."

Brian wrote down his new, more realistic thoughts, and committed them to memory. He wrote them down on an index card that he would take with him on the airplane.

Brian prepared to use the "experimental method" as a way to attack irrational thoughts that he could not combat with shear logic. For example, for the thought, "I'm losing control," he would ask himself, "If I were losing control, could I read the in-flight magazine?" He would then test this by reading the magazine.

Brian decided that he would make a point of striking up a conversation with the person next to him or across the aisle. He believed that this would help distract him from any unpleasant physical sensations. He also decided that he would listen to relaxing in-flight music if available.

During one session, I led Brian in a relaxation/ visualization exercise. Then, while he was relaxed, I had him imagine going on a flight and remaining calm and relaxed the whole time.

Brian worked very hard, but we still could only fit in a few appointments before the Thanksgiving season. One night before Thanksgiving, I was checking my voice mail and there was a message from Brian. "Dr. Hibbs! I just landed in New York. It was a great flight!" I saw him again after the holidays. All six flights had gone well. His fear of flying was gone!

Tips for Overcoming the Fear of Flying

1. Use deep breathing, relaxation, and visualization to reduce the intensity of physical arousal.

2. If you experience physical arousal, re-label it as harmless and temporary.

3. Prepare a list of realistic thoughts to counteract the irrational frightening thoughts.

4. Prepare a list of activities to help you use the "experimental method" to challenge frightening thoughts. Read the in-flight magazine or turn the air vent nozzle.

5. Think of ways to occupy your mind through reading or mental exercises.

6. Engage fellow passengers in conversation.

7. Distract yourself by taking note of your physical surroundings or observing the passengers and crew. Be curious about them.

8. Listen to relaxing music.

9. Make a recording of your relaxation/visualization exercises and your realistic thoughts and listen to them during the flight.

10. During the flight, focus your attention and what you plan to do when you arrive.

If you apply these techniques for yourself, you might find you no longer dread flying. However, if you find it too difficult to apply these skills on your own, a skilled CBT specialist can help you. Have a great flight!

Chapter Nine

FREEWAY PHOBIA
THE FEAR OF HIGHWAY DRIVING

When Teresa first came to see me, she was extremely frustrated and upset. She and her husband had purchased a beautiful home in a small town some 30 miles from Atlanta. Unfortunately, her job was in an area much closer into the city. The most direct way to get to work was to take several limited-access highways. However, after a few harrowing trips on Atlanta's daunting freeway system, she was much too frightened to venture on it again. This left her no choice but to take a long convoluted route on surface streets. This turned what should have been a 30-minute commute into a 2½ hour ordeal. Because of this, Teresa was chronically late for work, and she often called in sick. She became depressed. She loved her job and didn't want to lose it. However, she also loved her new home. What was she to do?

Like the fear of flying, the freeway phobia is really a variation of panic disorder. Think what it's like to drive on a busy limited-access highway. You travel at a high speed, there are multiple lanes of cars around you, and you can only get off the road by taking an exit. On a regular surface street, you can always pull off the road or turn into a driveway or parking lot. Not so on a freeway. It is that element of being "trapped" and not able to easily get off the road that makes freeway driving so scary for many people.

In addition, since the driver is actually operating the car, the fear of fainting, "freaking out," or "losing control" creates the fear of an accident. This adds an extra element of danger to his or her fear. Losing control in an airplane would be embarrassing, but losing control while driving on a freeway could be fatal.

Like most anxiety problems, freeway phobia is perpetuated by a faulty belief. The physical symptoms that are part of a panic attack create the illusion that the person is "losing control." In fact, although people in the midst of a panic attack often "feel" like they're losing control, they never actually lose control.

The trick to overcoming freeway phobia is to develop confidence that you can maintain control of your vehicle even if you experience the physical arousal that accompanies a panic attack.

Many of the techniques used to overcome panic attacks (Our time-honored Three C's) are also helpful in defeating freeway phobia. As always, the regular practice of deep abdominal breathing will increase your confidence and can be helpful when you begin to get anxious.

Learning how to reinterpret your physical sensations is also very helpful. If you can remind yourself that these sensations are harmless and will soon pass, you may find that your anxiety stays within manageable levels.

It is helpful to identify any distorted thoughts that are adding to your anxiety. Common examples of these are, "I'm going to pass out and cause an accident," or "I'm going to lose control and cause an accident." Learning how to challenge these thoughts will help you develop more rational thoughts such as, "I feel very uncomfortable, but these physical symptoms do not cause fainting," and "I feel very uncomfortable, but I can control my car."

However, even with deep breathing and rational thinking, the overwhelming fear of losing control is often very difficult to overcome. The most powerful way to attack that fear is through the "experimental method."

As mentioned in the chapter on panic attacks, the experimental method gives you the opportunity to "test" your irrational thoughts. In the case of freeway phobia, you will need to test your belief that you are losing control of your car. To begin, think of ways that you can be "in control" while you are driving. You can gradually lower or raise your speed, check your mirrors, change the radio station, or adjust the air conditioning.

To attack her freeway phobia, Teresa developed her own "menu" of such behaviors. Whenever she felt the onset of a panic attack, she would demonstrate that she was in control by engaging in one of these behaviors. By changing the radio station and looking in her mirrors, she was able to convince herself that she had adequate control of her car.

However, even after she was well prepared, Teresa did not tackle her rush hour commute right away. Instead, she attacked her fear in small steps. She started by going out on a Sunday morning to a relatively quiet stretch of highway. At first her husband rode with her. She drove from one exit to the next. Then she drove for two exits, then three, and so on. After a while she was confident enough to drive short distances without her husband. The next weekend she and her husband ventured out on Saturday morning when there was more traffic. Again, she took this on in small steps, first with her husband in the car and then by herself.

In this way, Teresa was eventually able to master her fear of the freeway and was able to take her daily commute to work with no problems.

In a few very severe situations, my clients have hired professional driving instructors to work with them for the first few steps. Since driving lessons are usually given in dual-control cars, they felt relieved to know that a professional could take over if they lost control. From there, they would move on to driving with a loved one and eventually by themselves.

Tips for Overcoming Freeway Phobia

1. Practice deep abdominal breathing while you are relaxed. This will give you confidence that breathing will help reduce the physical symptoms that accompany anxiety.

2. If you experience physical arousal, remind yourself that it is not harmful and will pass. Learn not to fight this sensation, but rather, just ride it out.

3. Memorize rational thoughts to counteract distorted thinking. This might include thoughts such as, "I feel uncomfortable, but I can control the car," "I'll just ride this out, and I'll be fine."

4. Use the "experimental method" to challenge your faulty belief that you will lose control of your car. Make a "menu" of action steps such as adjusting your speed, and checking your mirrors.

5. Take small steps to get comfortable on the freeway. Start with someone else in the car and/or on low traffic days. Gradually work up to your goal.

6. If necessary, hire a professional driving instructor to give you added security during the early phases of your recovery program.

These steps have helped many individuals overcome freeway phobia. Again, if you do not want to tackle these steps on your own, consult with a CBT specialist.

Chapter Ten
SOCIAL ANXIETY

Of all the things to be afraid of, it seems particularly tragic to be afraid of other people. After all, in our civilized society most people don't mean us bodily harm, so there's no reason to feel "unsafe" around them. Yes, people can be critical and judgmental, but their critical comments say more about them than about us. Most people are usually decent and as eager for us to like them as we are for them to like us.

Nevertheless, about six million Americans suffer from social anxiety severe enough to qualify for the diagnosis of Social Anxiety Disorder. Millions more suffer from a level of social anxiety that might be somewhat less severe but still detracts from their happiness and fulfillment in life.

According to the Diagnostic and Statistical Manual for Mental Disorders (DSM-IV) of the American Psychiatric Association, Social Anxiety Disorder is characterized by a "marked and persistent fear in social or performance situations in which embarrassment might occur. Exposure to the social or performance situation almost invariably invokes an anxiety response."

Feared situations might include parties, business meetings, or speaking to authority figures such as bosses or college faculty members. Even less clearly "social" situations such as standing in a checkout line or using a public restroom might be feared because the person perceives that others are observing him or her.

Most of us might experience discomfort in some social situations. If we go to a party where we know few people, we might feel a bit awkward and self-conscious. However, we would probably look around for a familiar face, figure out how to join in a group conversation, or introduce ourselves to a stranger. We might not have a great time, but we would manage to get through it. We might even make a new friend.

However, if you have significant social anxiety, you probably will avoid the party. The idea of being in a room with unfamiliar people would strike terror. You would imagine that people would notice how uncomfortable and anxious you are. You would perceive them as confident and outgoing, while you imagine that they see you as a "loser."

Many people fear public speaking, but if their job requires it, most people will get themselves to do it. However, people with social anxiety would not accept a job that had the slightest possibility of requiring public speaking.

For example, Jonathan had a dead-end job for a large government agency. About twice a year, he was asked to review the latest policy manual and briefly outline the changes for a small number of his fellow employees. Jonathan was always asked to do this because everyone knew that he understood the policy manual much better than any of his peers. His supervisor always gave him several weeks' notice of this assignment. The supervisor thought he was being nice, but it just meant weeks of agony for Jonathan. He would fret and lose sleep for days before the presentation. He would consider calling in sick or even resigning his job. Finally, with the help of some Xanax, he would somehow get himself through the presentation.

Apparently, Jonathan always did a good job, and no one else was even remotely aware of how miserable he was. He considered asking his supervisor to excuse him from this exercise, but he was too anxious to approach him.

Jonathan was very bright and certainly capable of moving up the ranks in his organization. However, he consistently resisted promotions for fear that a higher position would mean even more presentations.

Jonathan's anxiety went well beyond his fear of public speaking. He rarely spoke to his co-workers; he never attended social events, and he had not made a new friend since college.

I mentioned Paul in Chapter One. He was the fellow who wouldn't work in his yard or attend church. Paul imagined that other people would judge him negatively for even the most insignificant matter. To Paul his less-than-perfect yard and limited wardrobe were the source of completely unwarranted embarrassment. Paul was in fact a very pleasant and likeable young man. Unfortunately, he rarely let people get to know him.

Mind Reading

Back in Chapter Five, we explored how **thoughts** contribute to anxiety. We learned that certain thinking habits such as "fortune telling" and "catastrophic thinking" always underlie our anxiety.

Social anxiety is a little different. The primary thinking habit underlying social anxiety is "mind reading." That is, we are thinking about what other people are thinking of us. Although there is no way to really know what other people are thinking, we assume that their thoughts about us will be negative.

Here's a common scenario. You are invited to a business-related reception. You feel obliged to attend even though you don't expect to know many of the people there. You enter the room and see groups of people gathered in small clusters. You scan the room for familiar faces. Everyone you know seems to be locked in conversation with someone else. There seems to be no way to casually slip into a cluster without drawing undue attention to yourself.

This is not a situation that anyone might relish, but if you suffer from social anxiety, it's a nightmare. So, what are you thinking? Chances are it's something like, "Oh no, I don't know anyone here. They notice that I'm not talking to anyone. They think I don't have any friends. No one wants to talk to me. I look so out of place. They think I'm a big loser."

Mind reading is almost always at the core of social anxiety. Jonathan thought his co-workers would disapprove of his presentation while Paul worried about others' thoughts about his lawn and wardrobe.

It's like the mission is, "I have got to make all of these people like me. They must see me as relaxed, confident, intelligent, funny, attractive, etc." Social events are like "performances," and we fear getting bad reviews.

How much control do we really have over the thoughts of other people? It's probably not very much. No wonder we're anxious. We're trying to control something that we have little control over.

So, what are other people really thinking? In fact they're probably concerned about what we think about them. Socially anxious people find this hard to believe. We are so focused on what others are thinking about us that it's hard to believe that others actually care what we think of them.

So, if you want to be rid of your social anxiety, you will need to overcome your habit of negative mind reading. You will have to change your mission.

Changing Your Mission

This prescription for social anxiety seems too simple to be true. Nevertheless, when my clients have been able to grab hold of this idea and apply it, it has changed their lives for the better. Remember, if you're anxious in a social situation, you are trying to control something over which you have little control. You have made it your mission to get these people to feel good about you.

To get over social anxiety, you have to change your mission. You are no longer trying to get them to feel good about you. *Your mission now is to make them feel good about themselves.*

I'll get to the specifics of how to do this in a moment, but I want you to let this idea settle in for a moment. You are anxious because you are "self-conscious." You are focused on yourself and how you are coming across to others. The key is to become "other-conscious" by being genuinely interested in them. Get the focus off of yourself, and you might be amazed at how comfortable you become. *Again, the key is to change your mission. You are no longer trying to get them to feel good about you. You want them to feel good about themselves.*

The best way to change your mission is to actively engage others in conversation. What do you talk about? Them! When I first meet people, I try to see how long I can go before I have to talk about myself. I have been in conversations in which I said almost nothing about myself. Nevertheless, these conversations have generally felt very comfortable and relaxed. Why? Because I did everything I could to make the other person feel comfortable and important.

The secret to changing your mission is to ask questions. You can ask close-ended questions that can be answered in one or two words. Examples might include, "Do you live here?" "Do you like going to school here?" "Do you have children?" Since these questions are fairly easy to answer, it's good to start with them.

However, to keep the conversation going, you might want to ask some open-ended questions. These are questions that require a longer answer. Examples of open-ended questions might be, "How do you like living here?" "What do you especially like about your job?"

If you aren't sure what to ask about, there are three topics that are usually appropriate. These topics spell the word FOR.

F is for "family." Good questions include, "Are you from this area? Where did you grow up? Do you still have family there? What brought you to this area? How do you like it here? Do you have a family? How old are your children? Where do they go to school?"

O is for "occupation." "What kind of work do you do? How do you like it? How did you choose that career? What kind of training do you need to work in that field?"

R stands for "recreation." During the course of the conversation, the person might mention that they play tennis or love to go to antique stores. This will give you an opening with questions like, "How did you first get involved in that? What do you like about it?" Most people are more than happy to talk about their interests and hobbies.

Although it helps if you share some of the other person's interests, it is not necessary. In fact, I have had some of my best conversations with people with whom I had little in common. All it takes is a little curiosity. For example, since I live in the Southeastern U.S., I will also talk with men who are avid deer hunters. Quite frankly, the thought of sitting out in the cold waiting to shoot Bambi's mother does not appeal to me. However, when I ask a hunter why he likes it, he will talk about how beautiful and quiet the woods are in the morning. I am not ready to take up the sport myself, but I have listened to enough men rave about it that I certainly understand why they love it.

Core Beliefs in Social Anxiety

Whereas "mind reading" seems to be the most common thinking habit in social anxiety, there are several core beliefs that seem to underlie their surface thoughts. Here are a few that I have noticed.

Everyone who meets me must think well of me.

Of course, we don't want to go out of our way to offend others, and it's always good to be helpful and considerate of other's feelings. Howcvcr, socially anxious individuals have a concern that goes well beyond that. They cannot bear the thought that anyone might have even the mildest negative thoughts about them.

You may notice that there is also an element of "should" and "all or none" thinking in this core belief. Not only "must" everyone like me, but also they must "everything" about me. If anyone dislikes anything about me, they totally dislike me.

I always urge my clients to challenge this core belief. Although it is unfortunate if someone doesn't like you, is it really all that bad? As long as you are treating others honorably, do you really have to worry about what people think of you?

Think about some of the most embarrassing experiences that you have ever had. I'm sure they were very distressing at the time, but did all your friends abandon you because of it? Have you been completely unable to make friends since then?

As I look back at situations where I felt embarrassed—even humiliated—in the past, I now almost see them as blessings. They gave me the opportunity to see that my world did not end even if people saw me in a very negative light.

If people think badly of me, they will spread the word.

If it isn't bad enough to assume that others are thinking badly of us, we compound our misery by imagining that this negative information will somehow spread to everyone who knows us. This is sometimes called the "wildfire fallacy" because we believe that the negative opinions of us will spread like wildfire to everyone who knows us. Yes, people do gossip, but most people have more important things to do than to make sure that everyone is aware of our every misstep or misfortune.

Way back in Chapter One, I mentioned Paul, the man who wouldn't go out into his yard. He imagined that his neighbor with the perfectly groomed lawn would look down on him for his less-than-perfect lawn. Not only that, he imagined that his neighbor would talk about him and that the sorry state of his yard would be on everyone's lips.

It took a lot of "talking back" to his automatic negative thoughts before Paul was able to let go of this irrational fear. In time, he was able to enjoy working in his yard, and he even regularly struck up conversations with his neighbor, who turned out to be very nice and not the yard critic he imagined her to be.

My worth is based on the opinion of others.

In my work with clients with social anxiety, I bump up against this core belief continuously. It is so sad to see good people needlessly suffer because they are so concerned with public opinion or image.

To be honest, I used to live by this belief myself. Of course, I wouldn't have been able to admit it, not even to myself. Nevertheless, as I recall the anxieties that I have experienced over the years, I'm sure that this unfortunate core belief was a factor in many of them.

Now, I see things quite differently. I would still prefer that people like me rather than dislike me. I still try to treat all people with courtesy and respect. However, I do those things because they're the right things to do, not in order to gain approval. As long as I perceive myself acting in an honorable manner, I don't concern myself with whether other people like it or not. As one wise person put it, "Other people's opinions of me are none of my business."

The Feared Fantasy Technique

This is a wonderful therapy technique for attacking social anxiety that I learned from CBT pioneer, Dr. David Burns. The basic idea is to attack many of the irrational thoughts that underlie social anxiety by taking them to a ridiculous level.

I'll go back to the case of Paul, my client who was reluctant to go out into his yard. Since he imagined that his neighbor thought all these negative things about him, we decided to imagine a conversation in which his neighbor actually voiced all of these negative thoughts directly to him.

So, we set up a role-play in which he played the neighbor, and I played him. I told him to attack me for my poorly groomed yard. He was to be merciless—much worse than anyone would actually be. I would role-play him and respond to his criticism.

Our role-play went something like this:

Paul (as the neighbor): "I see that you're lawn isn't in very good condition."

Me (as Paul): "Oh, you're so right. I'm not very happy with the condition of my lawn."

Paul: "My lawn is much nicer than yours."

Me: "You're so right. You've got the nicest lawn in the neighborhood."

Paul: "I really can't respect anyone who doesn't keep his lawn."

Me: "You seem to have some pretty high standards about who you respect."

Paul: "Your lawn is so bad that I don't think you should be allowed in this neighborhood."

Me: "Well, I would move, but no other neighborhood will let me in."

When I made that last response, Paul broke into laughter. He could finally see how absurd his fears were. Any objective person could see that it was the imagined critical neighbor that was being unreasonable.

After this role-play, Paul and I switched parts. This time, he played himself and I was the critical neighbor. But this time, Paul was armed and ready for the criticism. Shortly after this session, Paul was ready to venture out into his yard and actually meet the neighbor who certainly wasn't the unreasonable person who had been portrayed in the role-play.

Self-Disclosure

When people are anxious in social situations, they often believe that they must hide their discomfort. They imagine that any sign of anxiety will cause others to judge them negatively. Obviously, this kind of thinking increases self-consciousness and only adds to the anxiety.

Many of my clients have benefited from taking a different approach. Whenever possible, I have coached them to be open about their anxieties. At parties, I encourage them to say things like, "I love parties but I tend to get a little nervous with new people." When preparing to speak to a group, I might suggest that they say something like, "I'm delighted to be here, but I must admit to being a little anxious about speaking with you. I'm not a natural public speaker."

Many clients are initially horrified at this idea. "I couldn't possibly admit that. What would they think of me?" But when I am able to persuade them to try it, they are often amazed at the results. They usually find that most people are not judgmental at all, and many empathize with them.

I remember a client who was dreading an upcoming business meeting in another state. He was particularly worried about a reception that was always held for the employees. In the past he had always been miserable at these events. He would skip it, but there was considerable pressure for all employees to attend.

As we explored options, I suggested that he find someone else who looked uncomfortable, introduce himself, and say something like, "These things make me so nervous." He didn't like this idea, but since we couldn't come up with anything better, he agreed to try it.

The next time I saw him, he was ecstatic. As recommended, he spotted someone who wasn't talking to anyone, introduced himself, and said, "These receptions make me so uncomfortable." Clearly relieved to have someone to talk with, the other man said, "Me, too. I hardly ever know anyone here." As the two of them chatted about how much they disliked the receptions, two other people who had overheard them joined the discussion. Everyone agreed that the annual receptions, although good for business politics, were not much fun. The four of them hit it off so well that they decided to leave early and have dinner together. My client had a wonderful time and made three new friends.

Tips for Overcoming Social Anxiety

1. Regularly practice your deep abdominal breathing during times you're already relaxed. This will give you

the confidence to use this technique in potentially stressful social situations. Since we're always breathing anyway, no one will notice if you take a few deep and slow ones. This will help you calm down, slow down, and think more clearly. (Calm your body)

2. Remember that social anxiety is always caused by our desire to make others feel good about us. Change your mission to trying to get other people to feel good about themselves. This will help you take the focus off of yourself and on to them. You'll be amazed at how much better that feels.(Correct your thinking)

3. Engage other people by asking questions, particularly open-ended questions that elicit a longer response. Ask questions that focus on family, occupation, and recreation (FOR). (Confront your fears)

4. Challenge your "mind reading" thoughts. Don't automatically assume that others are judging you. Treat other people honorably and then let go of any need to control how they think about you. (Correct your thinking)

5. When appropriate, use "self-disclosure" to let others know that you're anxious. It will disarm most critics and you'll immediately feel more relaxed. (Confront your fears)

Social anxiety is a particularly sad condition. Human beings were not put here to be frightened and intimidated by each other. We need to respect and care for other people but never give them the power to unduly control our behavior or how we feel about ourselves. Fortunately, regular use of the Three C's can help to greatly reduce social anxiety.

Chapter Eleven
WORRY

Not everyone has panic attacks or is afraid of flying, but everyone worries from time to time. When worry becomes excessive, chronic, and interferes with a person's ability to function, psychiatrists label this condition Generalized Anxiety Disorder (GAD). GAD is one of the most commonly diagnosed psychiatric disorders. Even if worry doesn't reach the level of GAD, life could be so much more enjoyable if we could find effective ways to overcome worry. Fortunately, the principles to help us understand the more serious anxiety disorders also help us overcome common worry.

Martha was 65 years old and had been a widow for many years. She was in good health, had many friends, was active in her church, was financially secure, and had good relationships with her grown children. Nevertheless, Martha was constantly worried. She worried about her health, finances, natural disasters, terrorism, and the well being of her children. If there were thunderstorms, she worried about tornados. If there were any mention of terrorism in the news, she worried that she would be a victim of an attack. Each therapy session brought a fresh batch of worries.

As her therapist, my first task was to listen to her with respect and take her worries seriously. I might be tempted to say, "Martha, that's silly. There's no reason to worry about that!" But, that wouldn't help her at all. After all, her well-meaning family and friends have been telling her not to worry for years. Saying, "You don't need to worry about that," only reinforced the worry.

Martha knew that most of her worries were unreasonable, but she felt powerless to control them. Even though her constant worrying was making her life miserable, she could not stop it.

It's important to note that Martha's worries rarely led to any productive action. Her constant worry about her finances didn't lead to better money management, and her concern for her health didn't cause her to take better care of herself. So, it couldn't be said that her worry served any useful purpose.

Why we worry: trying to control the uncontrollable

If worry just makes us miserable and serves no purpose, then why do we do it? To answer that question, let's go back to Chapter One in which I outlined the only healthy function of fear—that is, to warn of real dangers and to motivate us to take preventive action. In this respect, the ability to think ahead and foresee potential danger could be a real lifesaver.

But no matter how much we prepare for danger, we cannot create a completely safe and trouble-free environment. Since much of life is beyond our control, we can be sure that bad things can and do happen. We worry because it gives us the false sense of having some control over unpredictable events. In fact, many people actually worry about not having anything to worry about.

One of the best ways to combat worry is to draw clear distinctions between those things over which we have some control and those things that we cannot control. The best model that I know for this comes from Stephen R. Covey in his classic book, *Seven Habits of Highly Effective People.*

Picture two concentric circles: a small circle in the middle, surrounded by a larger circle around it. Inside the smaller circle, write the words, "Circle of Influence." This refers to everything in life over which we have some control. Basically, this is limited to our own behavior, attitude, and how we respond to people and situations. Truth be told, our Circle of Influence is quite small.

The area outside of the inner circle refers to our "Circle of Concern." This includes everything that influences us, but over which we have no control. Here are some things that are in the Circle of Concern: the actions of others, external forces such as the economy or the current social and political climate. Even everything that we have done in the past falls within the Circle of Concern because there is nothing that we can do about it now.

Covey notes that effective people focus their attention on things that are within the Circle of Influence. In doing so, they become empowered and the Circle of Influence expands. On the other hand, ineffective people focus on things that they cannot control and in so doing, the Circle of Influence shrinks.

Here's a simple example. An unemployed client tells me that he cannot find a job because "the economy is bad," or "they won't hire people my age." This man is putting his attention on the Circle of Concern and focusing too much on things that he cannot control. As a consequence, he will be half-hearted in his efforts, and his belief that he "can't get a job," is likely to be confirmed.

A more effective approach would be to ask, "How can I increase my chances of finding employment in this economy and at my age? Do I need to get more training? Can I study the industry in which I'd like to work? Can I work on my resume or do some networking?" Obviously, someone who takes this approach will expand the Circle of Influence and will be much more likely to find employment.

So how does this model relate to worry? When we worry, we are usually focusing on things that we cannot control. It's much wiser to focus on those things that we can control. That way, we are much more likely to take appropriate action.

Maybe you are familiar with the famous Serenity Prayer, which is recited at Alcoholics Anonymous and other 12-step meetings:

> "God grant me the serenity to accept the things I cannot change, the courage to change the things that I can, and the wisdom to know the difference."

This simple prayer clearly illustrates the ideas in Covey's "Circles." Let's look at each line of the prayer:

"God grant me the serenity to accept the things I cannot change." In other words, since I cannot change anything in my Circle of Concern, I might as well just accept it and give it as little attention as possible.

"The courage to change the things that I can." Although I cannot change anything in my Circle of Concern, if I focus on my Circle of Influence, perhaps I can take effective action to deal with whatever challenge I am facing.

"And the wisdom to know the difference." I must continually be honest with myself about what I can control and what I can't. If I can do something about it, I need to do it. If I can't do anything about it, I need to let it go.

Three steps to overcome worry

Probably the first and most famous self-help guru of the twentieth century was Dale Carnegie, author of the classic *How to Win Friends and Influence People.* Not everyone knows that Mr. Carnegie wrote another book entitled *How to Stop Worrying and Start Living.* In it, he outlines his three-steps for overcoming worry. I first learned about these three steps about forty years ago. The steps are simple and even common sense, but in all my years as a clinical psychologist, I have never learned a better system for handling worry. Here are the three steps:

Step One: Imagine the worst thing that can happen. Rather than deny the possibility of a negative outcome, go ahead and face it. Figure out the worst possible outcome and get a clear picture of it.

Step Two: Accept that the worst thing could happen. This is the hardest step. We come to terms with the possibility things could turn out badly, and we accept anything that comes. Important questions to ask during this step are, "What would be the real consequences if the worst thing happens? How will I cope with those consequences? What will still be good in my life should the worst thing happen?"

Step Three: Try to improve on the worst thing. Try to prevent it if you can. Once you have emotionally accepted that the worst thing can happen, take whatever action you can to prevent it.

Here is a personal example that illustrates these three steps. During my college years, I sometimes got to the middle of the term and found myself way behind in my work. I had exams to study for and term papers that I hadn't even started. One term I became so anxious that I was on the verge of panic and couldn't focus on my work.

Fortunately, I had just learned Dale Carnegie's three-step process, so I put them to work. Step one: I imagined the worst thing that could happen. I thought about every course I was taking and tried to figure out my worst possible grade. I might make an F in a couple of courses but figured I would make at least a C in several others. I did the math and figured out that my worst possible grade point average would be something like 0.8. Although I thought it unlikely that I would do that poorly, I had to at least consider the possibility.

Then I went on to step two. I would emotionally accept that I might do that poorly. I asked myself, "What would be the real consequences?" Well, I would probably be placed on academic probation and my parents would be very upset. "How would I cope with those consequences?" Well, I would certainly do things differently next term. I would start writing papers earlier and devote more time to study. Concerning my parents, I would apologize to them and pledge to do better. If necessary, I would leave my car at home next term in order to demonstrate my determination to do better. "What would still be good in my life?" Actually, quite a bit. I would still be in college. My parents, although upset with me, would still love me and wouldn't write me out of their wills. I would still have my friends. My health was good. I could still enjoy music and the beauty of nature. Although I don't want to make such bad grades, I would survive if I do. I could now accept whatever happened, which greatly reduced my anxiety.

Then I went on to step three. I took steps to prevent the worst thing from happening. Now that I was calm enough, I immediately got to work. I studied hard and wrote my papers. Thankfully, my grades were always much better than I feared.

Over the years, I have relied on this simple model numerous times to help me get through difficult times. "Accepting the worst" doesn't mean passive resignation or fatalism. It doesn't mean that you will be happy if the bad thing happens. It just means that you will find some way to cope.

I realize that there are situations that are extremely difficult to accept, and I'm not saying that you can apply these three steps in every situation. Certainly, it would be very difficult to come to terms with our own impending death or the death of a loved one. Nevertheless, people are very resilient and can often maintain their inner peace in the face of terrible consequences. Once, I spent a terrible weekend afraid that my son had a terminal illness. It was a terrible thing to consider, but I worked very hard trying to come to terms with it. Of course I was still quite upset, but I was at least able to calm myself enough to do what I had to do. Blessedly, it turned out that my fears were unfounded.

Intrusive worries: The DVD model

Sometimes, worry becomes so intense and relentless that it dominates virtually every waking moment. Often during times of crisis, our thoughts can become so dominated by our worries that thinking of anything else is almost impossible. The more we try not to worry, the more worry plagues us. That's why we call such worries "intrusive." They pop into our mind against our will, and we feel powerless to prevent them.

I have found a simple technique that can often be helpful in overcoming these kinds of intrusive worries. I call it the DVD player model because it's based on the electronic device that most of us have in our homes.

Imagine that your mind is a large DVD. The disk contains everything that is recorded in your mind—all of your memories and everything you've ever learned. The video screen represents anything that is currently in your conscious awareness. For example, take a moment to imagine the front of the building you attended for high school. Until prompted, that image was on your disk but not on your screen. However, when I mentioned it, you were immediately able to access the image and place it on the video screen.

When we're plagued by an intense intrusive worry, it's like the frightening thought or image is constantly on our screen. When we try "not" to think the scary thought, it's like pressing the "pause" button on the remote control. Rather than ridding us of the thought, it just gets stuck in our mind. That is because the mind doesn't know how to "not" think of things.

For example, if I tell you to not think about a unicorn, what immediately comes to your mind?

Keeping with this DVD model, I suggest three alternative methods for dealing with intrusive worries. All involve imagining taking hold of the "remote control."

First option: change the channel. When plagued by an intense worry, take hold of the remote control and change the channel. That is, have a "menu" of more pleasant and positive thoughts or images available to switch to when you begin to worry. My clients have been very creative in coming up with their menu of alternative thoughts. Some switch to relaxing scenes of walking on the beach or hiking through a beautiful meadow. Some switch to pleasant memories or to exciting dreams for the future. Still others have positive affirmations or Bible verses ready. If you have more positive things to think about, you can often limit the negative impact of recurrent worry.

Second option: "view" the thing you're worried about but do it in "fast forward." "Rewind" it, and watch it again but in "fast forward." I recently worked with a client who was overwhelmed with worry about losing his job and experiencing financial ruin. Together, we worked out a vivid image of his worst fears. He imagined losing his job, his home, and his marriage. He ended up on the street holding a "Will work for food" sign. I coached him to watch this scene in fast forward, rewind it, and watch it again. After a while, the image that had terrorized him had become ridiculous and boring. He was no longer plagued by this worry.

Third option: "record" the worry for future viewing. Sometimes, we might feel the need to at least give some thought to what we're worried about. The problem is that an intrusive worry completely takes over and makes it impossible to think about anything else. Again, pick up the remote control and push the "record" button. In other words, tell yourself, "I need to think about this, but I don't need to think about it right now. I'll think about it later." Some of my clients have even scheduled a specific block of time in which they purposely worry about whatever is bothering them. Of course, when the designated time comes, they might forget to worry or decide to delay the worry further. In any case, they are taking control of a process over which they previously had no control.

Tips for overcoming worry

1. If worry triggers the physical symptoms of anxiety, use the time-tested techniques of deep breathing, relaxation exercises, and visualization to help calm the body.

2. Focus on things that are within your Circle of Influence, and let go of things that you cannot control.

3. Remember the Serenity Prayer. Take action on those things that you can control and accept those things that you cannot control.

4. Apply Dale Carnegie's Three-Step process for overcoming worry: 1. Imagine the worst. 2. Accept the worst. 3. Take steps to prevent the worst.

5. When coping with intense and recurring worries, use the DVD model. 1. Change the channel. 2. Fast-forward and rewind. 3. Record for future viewing.

As with all other anxiety problems, coping with worry involves the three basic principles of anxiety-reduction: 1. Calm your body. 2. Correct your thinking. 3. Confront your fears.

Worry is the most common form of anxiety problems. Let's go on to a less frequent problem, but one that has recently proved to be more common than experts once thought: Obsessive-Compulsive Disorder.

Chapter Twelve
OBSESSIVE-COMPULSIVE DISORDER

Few psychiatric conditions are more perplexing and troublesome than obsessive-compulsive disorder or OCD. Yet, once OCD is clearly understood, it doesn't seem so hopeless, and it can be effectively treated.

For years OCD was a mystery disorder. Because people suffering from OCD have fears that seem so irrational and outlandish, it was often seen as a steppingstone to psychotic conditions such as schizophrenia. Now, we understand that this is not the case. For years, psychoanalytic therapists believed that OCD symptoms were outer manifestations of unconscious conflicts. Again, this explanation has not proved to be particularly helpful in treating the condition.

Now, OCD is seen as a cousin of the other anxiety disorders. As such, our Three C's (Calm your body, Correct your thinking, Confront your fears) are still helpful in overcoming this condition. As you will see, the ability to confront your fears is particularly important.

With advances in brain imaging and research in brain functioning, we are learning more about the neurological bases of OCD. I explain it to my patients this way. We all have a "danger switch" in the brain that signals when there is impending danger. In OCD, the switch sometimes gets stuck in the "on" position. When this happens, random thoughts such as "I wonder if there are germs on my hands" become triggers for intense anxiety. Most of us can disregard such thoughts. People with OCD are plagued by them. When such thoughts become repetitious and intrusive, we call them obsessions. When obsessions begin to take over a person's life, we call it OCD.

Although OCD has this clear physiological basis, psychological interventions are often very helpful in overcoming the condition. Again, treatment based on the cognitive-behavioral model seems to be the most effective—at least for now. There is even some evidence that suggests that effective cognitive-behavioral treatment for OCD actually leads to changes in brain functioning. This is exciting information that supports the strong interrelation between the mind and body.

What is an obsession?

In mental health, the definition of the word "obsession" is different from how it is used in everyday conversation. We might say that a teenage boy is "obsessed" with video games or that a young man is "obsessed" with his girlfriend. When used this way, the word suggests that the person enjoys thinking about the object of his obsession. This kind of obsession brings pleasure. This certainly isn't the case with the obsessions that occur in OCD.

To the mental health specialist, an "obsession" is defined as an intrusive, recurrent, unwanted thought or image that is very distressing. This type of obsession doesn't bring pleasure; it brings intense discomfort, anxiety, or even disgust. People may resist their obsessions, but the harder they try, the more the obsessions plague them.

My client, Susan, was obsessed with mold and mildew. Although she had been repeatedly reassured that they posed little danger, she was plagued by fear of being "contaminated" by them. She was so afraid of mold and mildew that she imagined that it was all around her. When she took a shower, any dark spot on the wall or tub, no matter how minute in size, was seen as the dreaded mold or mildew.

A teenage client, Thomas, was plagued by fears that someone had stolen his beloved baseball cards. Even though he had no rational reason to believe that his cards had been stolen, he constantly worried about it.

Another client, Kevin, was a devout man of faith, whose moral conduct was exemplary by any reasonable standard. He was also intelligent, well educated, and thoughtful; certainly not someone prone to irrational thinking. Nevertheless, Kevin was plagued by the terrifying thought that he had sold his soul to the devil and was headed for eternal damnation. Although this thought was completely contrary to the tenets of his faith, he couldn't free himself from it.

As you can see in these examples, obsessions usually involve some catastrophic outcome that is next to impossible but is seen as almost a certainty to the person with OCD. Well-intended assurance from others rarely provides much relief. At an intellectual level, Susan knew that she had little reason to fear mold and mildew. Thomas certainly understood that it would be impossible for someone to steal his baseball cards. Kevin had spoken to his pastor on several occasions who had patiently reassured him that his fears were unfounded. Nevertheless, none of these otherwise clear-thinking individuals could shake his or her obsession.

What is a compulsion?

Whereas an obsession triggers anxiety, a compulsion is an ineffective attempt to reduce the anxiety. Compulsions are usually behaviors, but sometimes they involve ritualistic thinking. Although the compulsion might offer some fleeting relief, it is extremely short-lived and the obsession usually returns, often stronger than ever.

When Susan was taking a shower, her obsessions about mold and mildew triggered intense anxiety. She would then engage in compulsive behaviors in order to reduce that anxiety. Before bathing herself, she would completely clean the whole shower stall. She might even clean the entire bathroom. When bathing herself, she would proceed in a very methodical manner. She would start at her right foot and carefully proceed up her right leg before washing her left foot and leg. If she had the obsession "Maybe I missed something," she would start over from the beginning. It was not uncommon for a shower to last 1-2 hours. Clearly, this was a major interference in her life.

Thomas countered his obsessions about his baseball cards by continually checking and rechecking the box where they were kept. He would look in the box very slowly and carefully in order to reassure himself that the cards were safe. However, as soon as he closed the lid, he would think, "Maybe I didn't really see them," and he would go and check again. He might take as long as 30 minutes going through his checking ritual before finally breaking away. Occasionally, this caused him to be late for school.

Kevin's compulsions were not behaviors. Instead, he would engage in ritualistic thinking in a vain attempt to reduce the anxiety caused by his obsession of having sold his soul to the devil. He would silently recite a certain prayer over and over. The prayer had to be recited "perfectly" or he would have to start all over again. A good portion of his life was devoted to this agonizing process.

In each of these cases, the OCD sufferer is plagued by a fear-provoking obsession and tries to reduce the anxiety by engaging in a ritualized compulsion. Unfortunately, each time they give in, their compulsions, become more strongly entrenched. They become trapped by their own thoughts and actions.

Varieties of OCD

OCD presents itself in several different ways. The most common obsessions concern excessive and irrational fears about dirt, germs, or toxic substances. I have already told you about Susan who worried about mold and mildew. In Chapter One, I mentioned Barbara who could not prepare food if there were any containers of cleaning products close by. Steven would not visit certain sections of the city because there were older buildings there that "might have asbestos." Steven would not allow his wife to drive a car that he believed might be "contaminated" from dirt from South Georgia where they use pesticides on the farms. People with these types of obsessions usually engage in excessive cleaning and washing compulsions.

Other OCD victims worry needlessly that their careless behavior will cause some calamity. They might fear that they will forget to lock doors, allowing a burglar to enter their homes. So, they might continually check and recheck doors and windows. Some might worry that they have forgotten to turn off appliances or unplug the iron, causing their houses to burn down. Still others have great difficulty driving for fear that they might have hit someone with their car. They might repeatedly retrace their route in order to ensure that they didn't hit anyone. They might then anxiously scan the local newspaper to see if there had been anyone injured in an auto accident. My teenage client, Thomas, is typical of such a "checker." Even though there was almost no chance that his baseball cards had been stolen, he wasted much of his precious time making sure that they were still there.

Some OCD sufferers are extremely uncomfortable if their personal items are out of order. They might spend hours arranging everything perfectly. They might line their books up from tallest to shortest. If even the most insignificant item is out of place, they will notice it immediately and become very upset. They might refuse to allow people to visit their homes for fear their perfectly ordered personal items might be disturbed. People with "ordering" symptoms usually don't have a specific catastrophe that they are trying to prevent. Instead, there is just a vague sense that something bad will happen if everything is not in its proper place.

Another type of OCD sufferer are those who needlessly fear that they have or will engage in some morally reprehensible behavior. I have already mentioned Kevin who feared he had sold his soul to the devil. I had one client who feared that he would someday turn into a child molester. Another happily married client feared having any sexual feelings toward anyone besides his wife for fear that he would have an affair. Thomas, my baseball card checker, also had fears that he would get involved in drugs, engage in delinquent behavior, and be sent to jail. It should be noted that Thomas was about as well behaved a kid as you would ever want. In fact, people with this type of OCD are always highly moral individuals who never ever actually engage in their feared behavior. The very fact that they are so distressed by their thoughts is a testament that it is not in their natures to engage in the feared behavior.

Yet another variety of OCD involves a fixation on certain numbers or patterns. I had one young client who had to do everything in fours. If he entered a room, he had to turn the light switch on and off four times. He had to count out his steps in groups of fours. I had another client who could not say or even think words that had a certain number of syllables. Likewise, he couldn't say or think sentences that had a certain number of words nor could he say or think sentences that ended with certain words. If he said or thought the "wrong" thing, he would immediately change it to something "right." As you can imagine, even the simplest conversation was exhausting. Like most OCD sufferers, this gentleman was bright and successful in other aspects of his life. Although clearly aware that his fears were irrational, he was still controlled by them.

As you can see, OCD presents itself in a wide variety of ways, and everyone with OCD has his or her own unique pattern of symptoms. A few points need to be made:

1. OCD goes well beyond normal worries and concerns. Most of us will double check our doors or wash our hands when we don't really need to. A person with OCD might check the doors a dozen times and wash their hands until they blister.

2. Although OCD sufferers often feel "crazy," there is no connection beyond OCD and more severe forms of mental illness such as schizophrenia. OCD sufferers sometimes truly believe their obsessions, but more often than not, they have at least some awareness that their fears are irrational.

3. OCD sufferers often experience tremendous shame and guilt about their disorder, which often prevents them from seeking treatment. This is extremely unfortunate because the disorder can now be very effectively treated.

Overcoming OCD: Calm Your Body

Just like with the other anxiety disorders, the Three C's play an essential role in recovery from OCD. Regular practice of the Calm Your Body skills will certainly come in handy. Getting over OCD is hard work, and you will no doubt experience some anxiety along the way. Deep breathing, relaxation exercises, and visualization will help you manage these anxious moments without resorting to compulsions. As you develop confidence in your ability to endure and manage anxiety, you will learn that you don't need to rely on compulsive behavior to feel better.

Correct Your Thinking

Your ability to Correct Your Thinking will also play an important part in your recovery. Specifically, your ability to manage and ultimately let go of your obsessions will be the key to your success. Here are some basic CBT principles for managing obsessions.

Re-label the obsession: An obsession triggers anxiety only because you fear that it might be true. However, once you understand that obsessions are merely "brain glitches" and have no basis in reality, you can recognize them for what they are. OCD specialist, Dr. Jeffery Schwartz, has coined the phrase, "It's not me, it's OCD" as a simple reminder of this fact. So when an obsession strikes, step back from it for a moment and re-label it. It's not "truth." It's just an obsession.

Accept the obsession: This might surprise you, but the best way to neutralize an obsession is to accept that you have it. So often, OCD sufferers respond to their obsessions with thoughts such as "Oh, no. This can't be happening again. There's something seriously wrong with me. I must be going crazy. I mustn't have these thoughts." As we have seen before, efforts to "not" think something only make you think it more. Paradoxically, if you just allow yourself to have the thought, it has less power over you, and you can let go of it sooner.

Delay the obsession: Do you remember the DVD model that was discussed in Chapter Eleven? One of the techniques in that model was "record for future viewing." One way to deal with obsessive thoughts is to just put them off for a while. Simply say to yourself, "I really don't have time to worry about that right now, I'll think about it in a half hour." Of course, after 30 minutes have passed, you can decide to put it off again if you wish. Like Scarlett O'Hara in *Gone with the Wind*, decide that you'll "think about it tomorrow," and you'll soon find that your obsessions no longer plague you.

Refocus away from the obsession: This is basically the same as the "Change the channel" technique in the DVD model. That is, you develop a repertoire of pleasant and positive thoughts and images that you can turn to when obsessions strike. So, when an obsession strikes, you can redirect your attention to a pleasant memory like your last trip to the beach. Or, you can turn your attention to other people or to your favorite hobby.

Change the obsession: Another way to reduce the obsession's power is to modify it in some way. As in the DVD model, you can "fast forward" and "rewind" your obsessions. You can also sing the obsession or write it down. Many OCD sufferers find that taking control of an obsession in these ways greatly reduces their anxiety.

Disregard the obsession: As we learned in Chapter Five, one way to disregard an anxiety-provoking thought is to imagine that it is being spoken by someone for whom you have little regard. This technique is often a big help with OCD. So the next time you have the thought, "You didn't lock the door," if you can imagine them being spoken by Archie Bunker or Homer Simpson, they will switch from scary to comical.

Bore yourself with the obsession: A scary movie is the most frightening the first time we see it. Watch it over and over again, and we eventually tire of it. There is a psychological process called "habituation" that explains why this happens. Our brains are wired to take special notice of anything that is new. However, once we become familiar with it, it has much less effect on us. We can apply this same principle to combat obsessions. CBT specialists often have their patients write their obsessions out. The patient is asked to describe their obsession with as much detail and emotion as possible. Then, the patient makes an audio recording of the obsession and listens to it over and over again.

Connie's OCD focused on thoughts and images of her cutting herself with a knife or other sharp object. Although she had no intention of harming herself, and she was always careful with sharp objects, she was plagued by the fear that she might someday "lose control," cut herself and bleed to death. I had her record a vivid description of how this might play out. She imagined that she became careless one day and impulsively cut herself. She slowly bleeds to death. Her husband comes home and finds her lifeless body, and her children grieve the loss of their mother. I had Connie listen to this tape for about 30 minutes a day for about a week. After that time, she was completely free of this obsession.

It takes courage for clients like Connie to purposely expose themselves to their frightening obsessions, but it's very effective. Obsessions have power because they come to us out of the blue. Everything changes if you have the thought on purpose. You control it; it doesn't control you.

Confront Your Fears

Confronting your Fears is a crucial component of recovery from OCD. In order to help patients confront their fears, CBT practitioners usually employ a process known as Exposure and Response (or Ritual) Prevention (ERP). As the name implies, ERP involves intentionally putting the patient in a situation that triggers anxiety. Then, rather than resorting to a ritualistic compulsion, the patient uses Calm your Body and

Correct your Thinking techniques to reduce anxiety in a different way.

In preparation for ERT, the therapist helps the patient develop a list of anxiety provoking situations. Situations are ranked on a 1-100 scale. Situations in the 20-40 range trigger mild to moderate levels of anxiety. Situations in the 40-70 range trigger moderate to severe levels of anxiety and are quite likely to lead to compulsive rituals. Situations above 70 are so anxiety provoking that the patient will almost always avoid them if possible. Once this list is developed, the therapist begins by helping the patient confront those situations that trigger anxiety in the 20-40 range. Once they can confront these situations with little or no anxiety, they will move to more moderate and then more severe situations.

My client, Daren, had fairly typical symptoms involving fears of germs and contamination. As a result, he wouldn't eat food with his fingers, and he would not allow his children to do so either. He wouldn't handle laundry—especially dirty underwear. He wouldn't touch trashcans nor would he use a towel or washcloth more than once. There were many items in his home that he would no longer touch because of previous "contamination."

Daren and I developed several different fear lists. For example, eating food with his fingers triggered anxiety at about the 40 level. Holding food in his hands and eating it all the way down to his fingers would trigger anxiety in the 60 range. Licking his fingers would elicit anxiety in the 80 range. Having his whole family eat a plate of nachos together would trigger anxiety at the 100 level. We developed similar lists for laundry, trash, towels/washcloths, and for touching "contaminated" items in his home. When possible, we would expose him to these situations during sessions (e.g. I had him eat finger food and lick his fingers during sessions). He also committed to "homework" assignments between therapy sessions during which he purposely exposed himself to increasingly difficult situations. Over a period of several months, Daren made great progress in reducing his symptoms of OCD.

For ERP to be successful, the patient needs to eventually confront situations at the very top of their fear lists. This takes courage but it is well worth it. One patient told me that it initially felt like stepping off of a ten-story building. However, he soon realized that he was merely stepping off of a ten-inch curb.

Other resources for OCD

There are a number of excellent books on OCD, and I recommend that you thoroughly educate yourself on your condition. The more you truly understand OCD, the easier it will be to overcome it. There are four books that I particularly recommend. *Brain Lock* by Jeffery Schwartz, MD, provides some interesting insights into the physiological causes of OCD. He also provides a simple four-step formula that helps you "correct your thinking" about your obsessions. This book is an excellent place to start.

Another book, *The OCD Workbook*, by Bruce Hyman and Cherry Pedrick provides detailed instructions on how to rate the severity of your symptoms and step-by-step instructions on how to attack them.

My favorite book for OCD adults is *Stop Obsessing* by Edna Foa and Reid Wilson. This simple little book clearly defines the different varieties of OCD and outlines many of the techniques for managing obsessions and resisting compulsions.

For parents of children with OCD, *Freeing your Child from OCD* by Tamar Chansky is an excellent resource. It outlines how to talk to the child about OCD and how a parent can coach the child to combat many of his/her symptoms. It also presents an innovative way for the child to think about scary obsessions. The child is told to imagine that a "bully" is trying to convince them to do "stupid things." However, the bully really has no power and doesn't know what he is talking about. The children are then taught to talk back to the bully and show him who the boss is.

Treatment works!

Clinical research has shown that both medication and cognitive-behavioral therapy (CBT) are effective in significantly reducing or even eliminating OCD symptoms. Most adult patients who I have treated with CBT have also been on medication at least at the beginning of treatment. Because effective treatment requires the patient to directly confront their fears, medication sometimes takes the edge off just enough to make treatment possible. Even if medication alone significantly reduces symptoms, I still recommend that the patient receive CBT. That is because CBT gives the patient tools to continue to effectively combat OCD even after medication is discontinued.

Interestingly, all of the children that I have treated for OCD have done very well with CBT alone and have not required medication. That is not to say that medication would not be helpful in some cases, and I wouldn't hesitate to recommend it if it were necessary. However, it just hasn't been necessary with the children that I have seen. I am not certain why this is so except I suspect that they are benefiting from earlier diagnosis and treatment. Now that OCD is more understood and is being recognized earlier, perhaps the next generation of OCD patients will be spared the years of misery endured by their elders.

If you think that you might be suffering from OCD, I urge you to seek help from an experienced therapist who practices CBT. Although most anxiety problems can sometimes be overcome without professional treatment, it's extremely difficult to tackle OCD on your own. For too many years, people with OCD have needlessly had their lives severely limited. Feeling hopeless and saddled with feelings of guilt and shame, they have not sought the treatment that could set them free. I hope this book encourages you to seek the help you need.

Chapter Thirteen
FINAL THOUGHTS

Most of this book has focused on the clinical aspects of anxiety recovery and the techniques of CBT. However, I want to step away from the purely clinical arena for a moment and briefly review three ideas that are just as relevant to anxiety recovery: courage, faith, and love.

Courage

Cognitive-behavioral therapy for anxiety may seem like a fairly technical, even mechanical process. It's hard to see how a concept like "courage" fits into the equation. However, it's a very important concept to understand. Courage is not the absence of anxiety. Courage is the willingness to experience anxiety but not let it limit your choices. "Feel the fear, but do it anyway," is the motto of the courageous person.

I am often asked to speak to professional organizations. Quite frankly, this sometimes requires courage. As soon as I accept the speaking engagement, my "automatic thoughts" start going. "I won't have anything meaningful to say. They won't like it. Yes, I've done OK before, but this time I'll really mess up." These thoughts begin to trigger my anxiety, and I have to apply the "Three C's" to overcome them. But, the pleasure that I get from speaking to groups far outweighs the little bit of anxiety that I experience in the process. However, I would have never known how much I enjoy public speaking if I had not developed the courage to try it the first time.

If you examine your own life, you will see that you have already shown courage many times. You started school, you started a new job, and you got married and had children. All major life transitions require courage, so you have shown it more than you realize.

A fearful person is often advised to "take courage." That's an interesting choice of words. It suggests that "courage" is something that we can "take" or "grasp hold of." People who struggle with anxiety often see themselves as "lacking courage." But courage isn't something you "have," it's something you "take hold of." Consistent application of the Three C's of anxiety recovery will actually help you develop courage. You will feel anxiety, but you will "do it anyway."

Faith

Religious faith doesn't make you immune to anxiety problems. Fear strikes believers and nonbelievers alike. However, I have observed that people of faith tend to fare a little better in tackling their anxiety problems. It's easy to see why this is so. If you believe in a loving and benevolent God, you will have a more hopeful outlook for the future. No matter how your current situation turns out, you know that God will be with you. That belief is bound to reduce your anxiety.

However, unhealthy religious beliefs can also contribute to anxiety. If you only see God as judgmental, condemning and just waiting to punish you for the slightest misstep, then you're bound to be plagued with excessive anxiety. It's certainly not my place to tell you what your religious beliefs should be. However, if your beliefs create more misery than security, more guilt than comfort, and more anxiety than peace, it's possible that you misunderstand the basic tenets of your faith. It might be helpful to have an open discussion with a trusted spiritual advisor.

Many of my anxious clients have a strong belief in a loving God. Sadly, however, these clients often condemn themselves for their anxiety. They say, "If I only had stronger faith, I wouldn't be anxious." I explain to them that overcoming anxiety is a skill, like driving a car or playing the piano. They haven't been able to overcome their anxiety, because they lack skill and knowledge, not because they lack faith.

Love

Ultimately, love may be the antidote for anxiety. By this, I don't mean simply romantic or sentimental love. Instead, I am referring to what the Greeks referred to as Agape love. This is the kind of love that allows us to truly accept others and to truly accept ourselves. This kind of love motivates us to be the best we can be and strives for what's best in others. There's a verse in the Bible that says, "Perfect love casts out fear." If we consistently adopt a loving attitude towards ourselves and others, it will be very difficult for anxiety to take hold of our lives.

My prayer for you and yours

Everyone experiences anxiety a little differently, but I hope that you can now see how the Three C's are an essential component to all anxiety recovery. Learn to Calm Your Body, Correct Your Thinking, and Confront Your Fears and you will be well on your way to being free of anxiety.

Maybe you have a friend or family member who needs this book. If so, I hope you'll pass it on to them. Maybe they will benefit and pass it on to someone else. However, please be patient with your friends and loved-ones if they don't take hold of these ideas immediately. Certainly, we can help each other overcome anxiety, but ultimately everyone has to tackle their fears in their own time. No one can do it for them.

I hope I have conveyed some sense of my passion and commitment to this subject. So many people resign themselves to living in fear and see no hope for anything better. That is such a waste. My prayer is that this little book has given you some encouragement to take on your anxiety problems and overcome them. I truly believe that no one has to be overly burdened by anxiety. Many people have conquered their anxiety. You can too!

BIBLIOGRAPHY

Beck, Aaron. Cognitive Therapy of Depression. New York: Guilford Press, 1979.

Burns, David. The Feeling Good Handbook. New York: Penguin Books, 1989.

Carnegie, Dale. How to Stop Worrying and Start Living. New York: Pocket Books, 2004.

Chansky, Tamar. Freeing Your Child from Obsessive-Compulsive Disorder. New York: Three Rivers Press, 2000.

Foa, Edna and Reid Wilson. Stop Obsessing! New York: Bantam Books, 1991.

Hope, Debra et al. Managing Social Anxiety: A Cognitive-Behavioral Therapy Approach. Graywind Publications, 2000.

Hyman, Bruce and Cherry Pedrick. The OCD Workbook. New Harbinger Publications, 1999.

Schwartz, Jeffery. Brain Lock: Free Yourself from Obsessive-Compulsive Behavior. New York: HarperCollins, 1996.

Wilson, Reid. Don't Panic: Taking Control of Anxiety Attacks. HarperPrennial, 1996.

Also by Dr. Hibbs:

Consider It Done: Ten Prescriptions for Finishing What You Start, iUniverse, 2004

To Contact Dr. Hibbs Concerning Either of His Books:

Stanley E. Hibbs, Ph.D.
1864 Independence Square
Suite A
Atlanta, GA 30338

Phone: 770-668-0350 x-224
Fax: 770-668-0417

Email: drhibbs@drhibbs.com

Web sites: www.drhibbs.com
www.dunwoodypsychologists.com